CONTENTS

EMBROIDERED PURSES

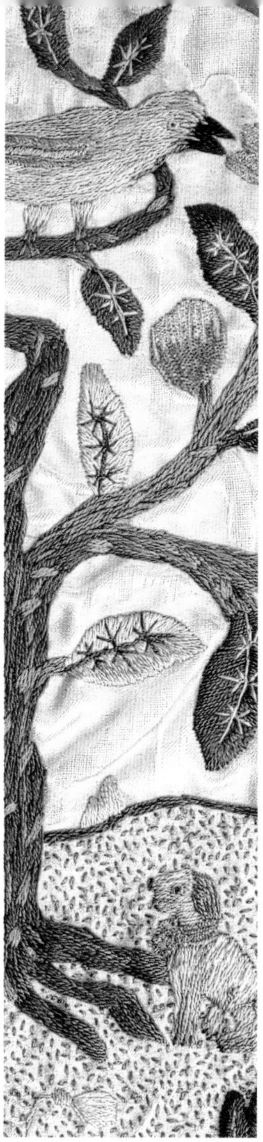

IN MEMORY OF SUE BARRETT

All drawings and illustrations by the author. All purses by the author unless otherwise stated.

First published 2004
Reprinted 2005

This paperback edition published in the United Kingdom in 2006 by
Batsford
151 Freston Road
London W10 6TH

An imprint of Anova Books Company Ltd

Photography by Michael Wicks and Peter Read

ISBN-13: 9780713490268
ISBN-10: 0 7134 9026 8

A CIP catalogue record for this book is available from the British Library.

10 9 8 7 6 5 4 3 2 1

Reproduction by Anorax Imaging Ltd, Leeds
Printed and bound by Kyodo Printing Co Pte Ltd, Singapore

This book can be ordered direct from the publisher at the website: www.anovabooks.com, or try your local bookshop

Distributed in the United States and Canada by Sterling Publishing Co., 387 Park Avenue South, New York, NY 10016, USA

Page 1: PAPER PHAETON PURSE
This purse was made with a drawing of a statue of Phaeton and his falling chariot in the Victoria and Albert Museum, London. The drawing was colour-photocopied, crumpled and inverted, then gently bonded to a base of butter muslin. This was then free-machine embroidered using black threads. The construction and lining were achieved in a similar way to folded purses (see chapter 5), with the addition of a circular base. The handle was created with pelmet Vilene, the shape echoing that of the purse and the texture deliberately smooth as a contrast.

Page 2: CHINESE PURSE
Embroidered with gold-covered thread and coloured silks in Pekinese stitch, this purse from China is a curiosity. Was it used to hold herbs or spices, incense or a scroll? Measuring only 13cm (5in) long, its dark blue silk background fabric has worn away in places.

Page 3: MYSTERY PURSE
This delicate purse, made of a grid of discs strung together with tiny pink beads, seems to have been made to commemorate Napoleon's expedition to Egypt in 1798.

EMBROIDERED PURSES

LINDA TUDOR

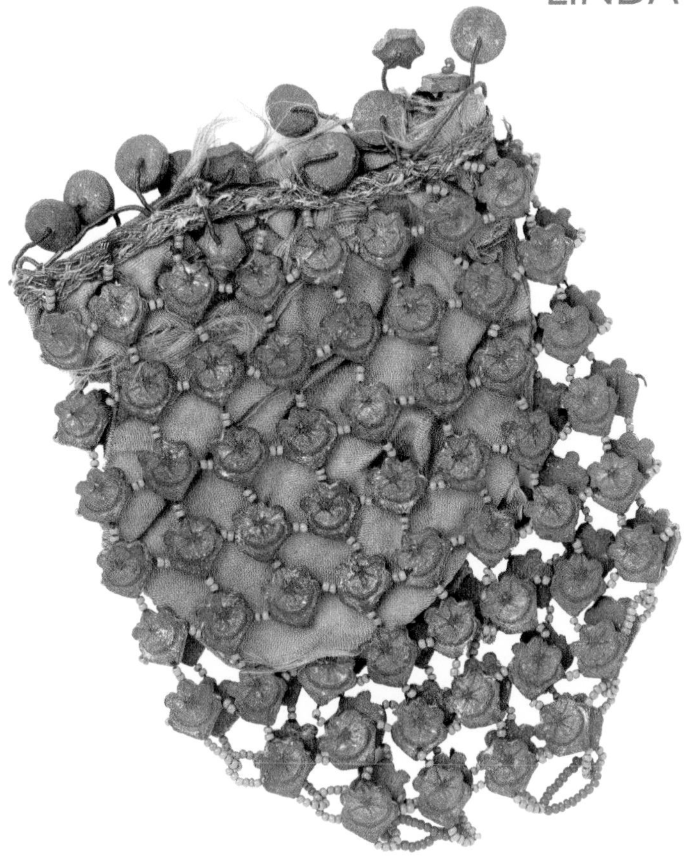

BATSFORD

ACKNOWLEDGEMENTS

I would like to thank all those artists who have so generously lent purses for the book: Hilary Bower, Jenny Bullen, Jennifer Collier, Emily Jo Gibbs, Lucy Goffin, Joss Graham, Sheila Jolly, Mie Iwatsubo, Maureen King, Joan Matthews, Jan Miller and Lucy Quinnell.

I would also like to thank the museum curators Lynn Szygenda and Katherine Carlton from the Embroiderers' Guild and Mary Alexander from the Guildford Museum for their help, and Dr Irving Finkle for his insights.

Also Muriel Best, Sian Martin and Rosemary Williams for their help, and my very good friend Dorothy Stapleton for generously sharing her expertise.

Last and by no means least, I would like to thank my family for all their support and especially my son Ben, whose patience in teaching me a fraction of his computer skills has been outstanding and without whom this book would not have seen the light of day.

'STUMPWORK' PURSE
Textiles have always been cut up and reused, and this purse is no exception. At first glance, the purse looks like a 17th-century piece of stumpwork, but the threads are similar to those of the 19th century and the animals have an Arts and Crafts feel to them. It is thought that the embroidery is a late 19th-century copy of a stumpwork piece of the 17th century, and must have originally been larger. It has been attached to a manufactured metal frame, with unfortunate consequences for the bug on the right.

PREFACE

The word 'purse' means different things in different parts of the English-speaking world. In Britain, a purse can mean a money bag and its contents, a small amount of money (perhaps as a present or prize) or a small pouch. In America, a purse is a much larger handbag.

For the purposes of this book, a purse is a small, precious container – an intimate, personal object, exquisitely decorated. Many are pure fantasy, one-off pieces designed as objets d'art and collected avidly, by those interested in fashion as well as by textile enthusiasts.

This book is about small bags, exquisitely embellished in a multitude of ways. After sections on the history of purses and examples from around the world, there are instructions on how to design and make purses, using a variety of construction methods from the simple to the more complex and many techniques for decoration.

I hope that you will be intrigued by the many examples shown here, both historical and contemporary, and, having mastered some of the techniques involved, will be inspired to design and create your own unique purse.

LUCY GOFFIN'S PURSE
This delicious purse, made by Lucy Goffin, was inspired by the shapes of boats. It measures 6.5cm (2½in) high and 12cm (4¾in) wide. Ottoman silk and dupion silk were stitched together in strips, alternating with covered piping and reminiscent of the wooden planking on boats. The purse is constructed in such a way that the joining of the component pieces creates a solidity that supports the shape. The insertion and chain stitches on each side are structural as well as decorative, as they hold the shape together. A covered button and loop provide a fastening.

INTRODUCTION

People have been creating purses for millennia. It seems that as soon as items became important or precious, purses were made to contain them. As far back as 2400 BC, the Assyrians carried medicine in bags called *naruqqu*. There are Babylonian words for 'bags for carrying textiles'. There is even an ancient word for 'a bag for carrying oil in the skin of a weasel'. Ancient Egyptians had no coins so they carried jewellery and other precious items in squares of cloth, tied at the corners. As containers of precious personal effects, these were no doubt marked in some way to personalize them, and it is not difficult to imagine the development of decoration, embellishments, handles and methods of fastening from these simple beginnings.

Herbs, spices, medicines, relics and ammunition, as well as alms, money, keys and seals of state, have all warranted safe-keeping, and over the centuries this has given rise to a huge variety of purses. Some were made for ceremonial occasions while others were for entirely private use, but all were vehicles for individual expression.

Occasionally, ancient purses survive and can be seen in museums. A collection of domestic purses can reveal much about women's lives. The shape, size and structure of purses changes with developments in costumes, with the changing needs in personal effects and the new opportunities and materials available to the maker. Occasionally, a purse may contain a remnant of the user's life, such as a coin, a dance card, part of an earring or a scrap of paper with a noted address. Older purses may still contain wool that was once scented, or gaming counters, worn smooth with use. These remnants are poignant reminders of the personal nature of purses. Made to enclose, a purse can contain our most private of possessions, concealing an inner space within a decorated exterior.

A 17TH-CENTURY PURSE
This early 17th-century purse is worked in or nué. In this technique, a gold thread (or sometimes a pair of threads) is laid over a design and couched down with coloured silks. The ground fabric is entirely covered with rows of painstakingly laid gold and the design is interpreted with the silks. The flower motifs with butterflies on each of the four sections of this purse are expertly embroidered, each motif fitting one of the four shield-shaped sides. A cord is drawn through slits in the fabric and it has two heavy tassels, worked over wooden forms on the drawstring. (Guildford Museum)

SWEET PURSE

For many people, the quintessential purse is the 17th-century 'sweet' purse. The one illustrated here, dated 1600–1625, can be seen in the British Galleries of the Victoria and Albert Museum, London. Some sweet purses contained perfumed powders to counteract bad odours, and others were made as special containers for exceptional presents. Many were regarded as so precious that they are mentioned in wills. This one was probably used by a woman as a sewing kit because there is an accompanying pincushion. The ground of linen canvas is covered with gobelin stitch in silver thread. Roses and violas blooming on coiling stems have been worked in tiny tent stitches in subtly graded coloured silks.

CHAPTER ONE HISTORY

Because of the delicate nature of textiles and their susceptibility to damp, sunlight and general wear and tear, there are few surviving examples of pre-medieval domestic purses. However, purses made to contain exceptional items, such as relics brought back from the Crusades or seals of state, do occasionally survive.

In Caen, in north-west France, a workshop set up by Mathilda, wife of William the Conqueror, was famed for its embroidered alms purses or 'tasques'. Commissioned by wealthy families, these purses were embroidered in metal threads and silk. Commonly used images included flowers, figures and coats-of-arms, and such purses were regarded as status symbols.

Seal purses were made for specific occasions and a variety of embroidery techniques were used, including appliqué. An example, to be found in Westminster Cathedral, is the seal purse of Edward 1, which was made in 1280 and displays applied lions on a shield-shaped purse. Professionals in organized workshops produced exquisite work during the 13th and 14th centuries, using underside couching and metal threads. Thereafter, the Black Death and the availability of imported brocaded silks changed the nature of English embroidery.

We can catch glimpses of more everyday purses in old tapestries, paintings and brass rubbings. These show ladies with drawstring purses hanging from their girdles, peasants with robust leather bags and rich merchants with money bags strapped to their belts. Variously made of leather or velvet, some of these bags were of the drawstring type, while others were stitched to metal frames to give more structure.

By the late 16th and early 17th centuries, the magnificent costumes of the Elizabethan court were festooned with elaborate embroidery. Purses, pomanders, keys and pincushions were hung from the belt and secreted in the folds of the skirt. Purses were made by domestic embroiderers as well as by professionals. These 'sweet' purses were small, square, made with linen or canvas and exquisitely embroidered in silk and metal threads. The designs, featuring formal flowers, leaves and insects copied from the herbals, bestiaries and embroidery pattern books that were newly available, were arranged within the shape of the purse. Some professionally made sweet purses were commissioned to enclose gifts of jewels or money. Their precious nature has resulted in the survival of many in superb condition, complete with cords and tassels and some with matching pincushions, all displaying wonderful workmanship. See drawing on page 11.

Gaming purses were designed to hold coins or counters. Some elaborately embroidered examples can still be seen in museum collections. They are circular, flat-bottomed and with short sides through which drawstrings pass for closure. Closely worked in gold and silver threads, some have the coats-of-arms of the owners worked on their bases.

AN ITALIAN PURSE
This purse, from the Guildford Museum, is in superb condition. Its construction, with four sections each shaped to form a flat base and shallow sides, suggests that it may have been made as a gaming purse. See also page 15. (Guildford Museum)

The end of the 17th century saw the development of 'pockets' that were sewn on tapes, tied around the waist and worn under voluminous skirts. A slit opening in the skirt corresponded to the opening in the pocket. For all the carrying capacity of the pocket, tiny novelty purses were also made, two examples of which are in the Museum of London. One has been created from walnut shells covered in silk and decorated with seed pearls and coral beads. Another example is in the shape of a frog with a drawstring opening for a mouth, seen below.

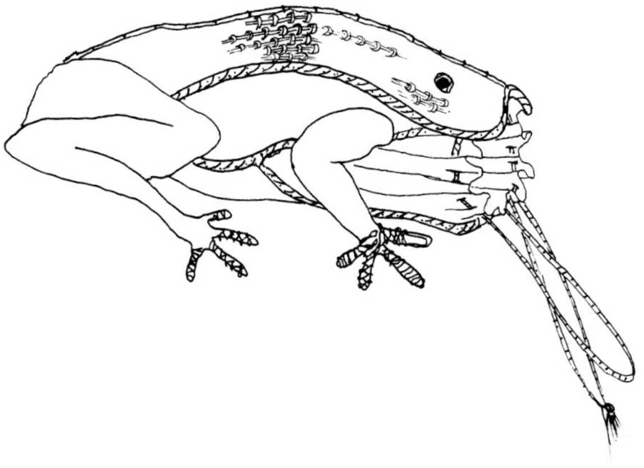

A 17th-century drawstring purse in the shape of a frog has been worked intricately in silver thread on cream silk. The whole is embroidered with detached buttonhole stitch and the stitching underneath is arranged in a diaper pattern. The mouth, with an olive green drawstring cord, forms the opening. The digits are stitched over bent wire in silver thread. It was probably used as a scent pouch.

The late 18th century saw skirts becoming narrower and, for the first time, a bag or 'reticule' became an essential fashion item. Often made of silk or velvet, these were gathered around the top edge with ribbons to tie around the wrist and were carried with fans. 'Stocking' or 'miser's' purses were made with a variety of techniques and were used by both men and women. They were long and tubular, with a slit in the middle of the length through which to insert coins. Two metal rings slid up to prevent the money from escaping from the ends. These were made and used well into the 19th century, with small refinements. Knitted or crocheted with beads, stocking purses were made from a silk that had a particularly hard twist and was specially manufactured for the purpose.

The wider crinoline skirts of the Victorian era saw a revival of chatelaines, which were made of leather or velvet and hung with chains from the belt. The rise in the popularity of printed magazines for ladies coincided with the growth in wealth of the middle classes. Needlework was regarded as a desirable pastime for leisured ladies and the purse was deemed an ideal item to show one's talents. Silk, satin and velvet were used, often to match the outfit. Indoor purses, outdoor purses, purses to hold visiting cards and purses to contain dance cards and pencils – all were embellished enthusiastically with silk, paint, beads, fish scales, beetles' wings, ivory, tortoiseshell and mother-of-pearl. Their variety ranged from highly coloured, heavily decorated purses with metal frames to delicately painted floral images in pale colours on paper-thin silk. Today, at antiques fairs and in collections, it is still possible to find purses that slavishly follow patterns and instructions printed in 19th-century ladies' magazines.

By the 1870s, leather handbags were introduced for daytime use, to accommodate the increasing number of personal items. Handmade, hand-embroidered and beaded purses continued to be made for evening use well into the beginning of the 20th century. By the 1920s, when shorter hemlines and beaded party dresses came along, clutch bags were the fashion for both evening and daytime use. Some were made professionally in Austria, using the new Art Deco designs that had just come into vogue. These were created to add to the decorative effect of an outfit, not necessarily to match it, and with the discovery of Tutankhamun's tomb, Egyptian-inspired decoration appeared on many. 'Pochettes' or clutch purses were also made in surprising shapes, including cars and cigarettes, symbols of women's new-found independence.

Today, there has been a revival of interest in beautiful purses, many made in the Far East. Others are collectors' items, made to be used only on special occasions. The variety of styles and materials used is vast and the desire to own something unique has meant that many purses are made as one-off works of art.

AN ITALIAN PURSE
Each section of this purse is embroidered with silk threads in satin, chain and long-and-short shading stitches. The twisting flowers and leaves, along with the occasional insect, are designed to fit within the satin panels. The panels are stitched together with braid over the seams. A drawstring passes through holes in the fabric at the top edge. *See also page 12.* *(Guildford Museum)*

English purses

a. CROCHETED DRAWSTRING PURSE
Only 10cm (4in) in each dimension, this crocheted, drawstring purse is lined with silk. The raised flowers were made separately and later sewn together. The purse is lined with mauve silk and was made in the 19th century, probably following a printed pattern.

b. PINEAPPLE PURSE
This purse was made between 1800 and 1820 and was knitted in cotton on a very fine gauge needle. Measuring only 11cm (4¼in) long, it was created to carry a dance card or perhaps just a handkerchief. It is decorated with tiny metal beads threaded onto the knitting cotton and worked into the structure. The top is embellished with minute white beads. A drawstring is passed through a series of holes, made especially for the cord.

c. COIN PURSE
This tiny purse, measuring 7.5cm (3in) long by 6.5cm (2½in) wide, was made to contain coins. Thousands of similar purses were made in the 19th century. Sometimes the surface was embroidered with beads and sometimes beads were threaded onto special 'purse silk', which was used to knit, crochet, knot or weave. Probably dating from around 1846, this example has been knitted and has loops of steel beads along the top to take a drawstring. Many such purses were formed over wooden or ivory purse moulds.

d. and e. MISER'S PURSES
Miser's purses were made in vast numbers during the Victorian era, as both men and women used them, and many patterns for their manufacture were printed in magazines. This red twill purse (d), from the Embroiderers' Guild collection, is unusual as it is made of fabric and is in two halves, seamed around the edge. Floral arrangements of beads adorn each side, with gold beads strung into four loops forming tassels at the ends. Many miser's purses were knitted, knotted or crocheted and, like the dark red example (e), incorporated metal beads and rings, which added considerably to their weight.

f. MAN'S WATCH PURSE
This home-made purse, resplendent with the Prince of Wales's feathers and motto, Ich Dien, *was made around 1859, following the publication of a pattern in a ladies' magazine. It was made to hang on the bedstead at night, with a man's watch stored inside. Some similar examples have a hole so that the watch face can be viewed through the front of the purse.*

g. WAISTCOAT PURSE
This silk-embroidered bag has been made from a man's waistcoat, the top being the original pocket flap. On cream silk, it is embroidered in satin stitch, stem stitch and French knots with floss silk threads. Sequins and satin stitch over card shapes have been worked around the edge. One wonders if the owner of the waistcoat was aware of its transformation.

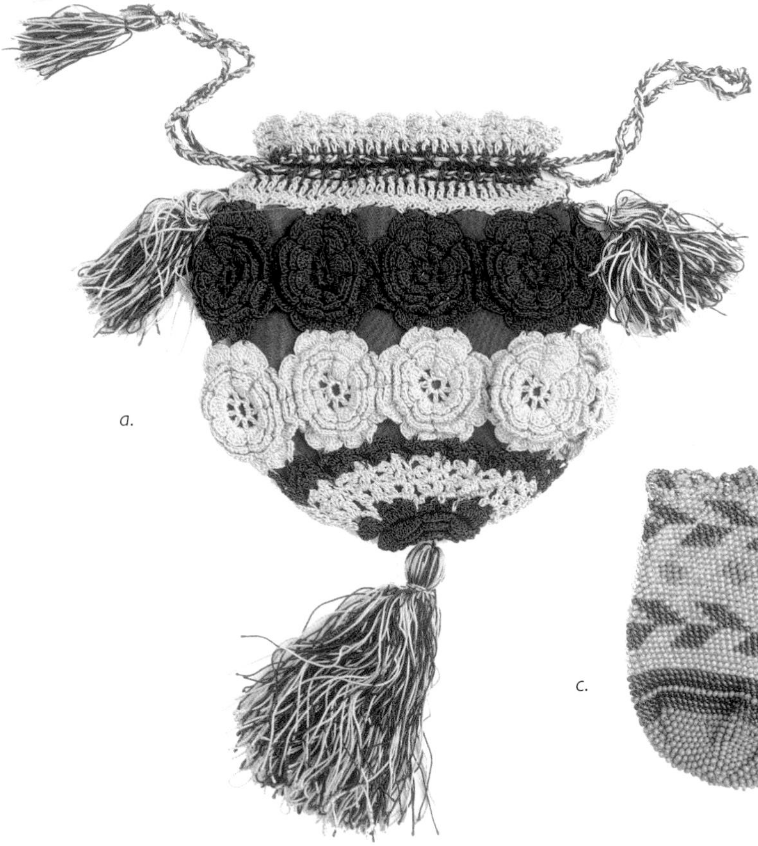

a.

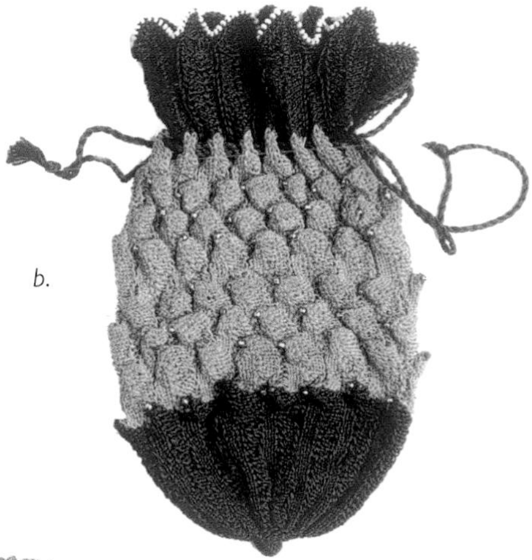

b.

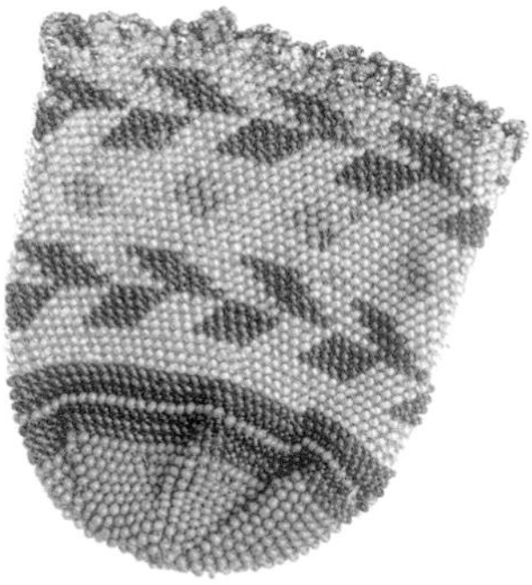

c.

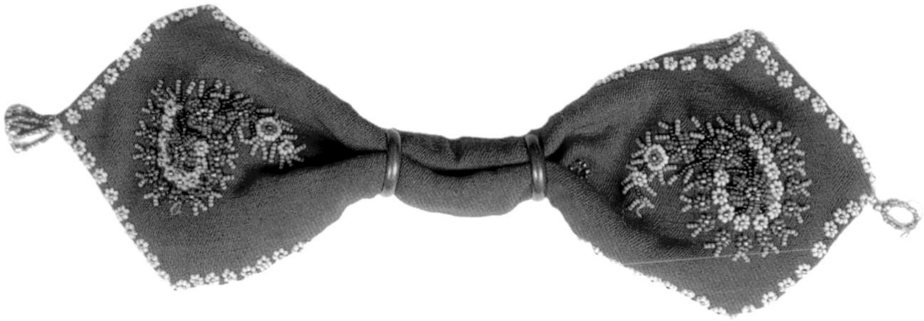

d.

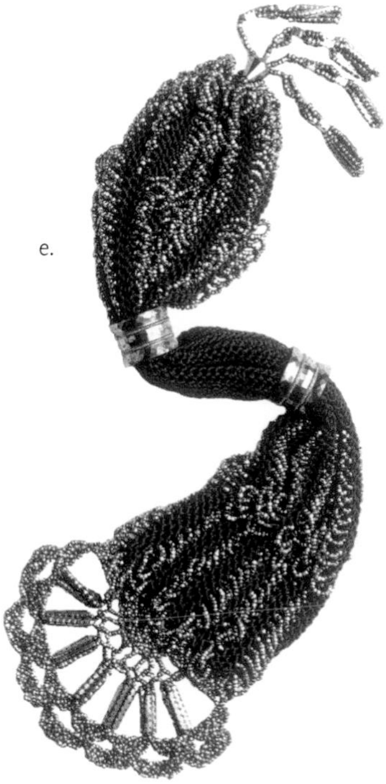

e.

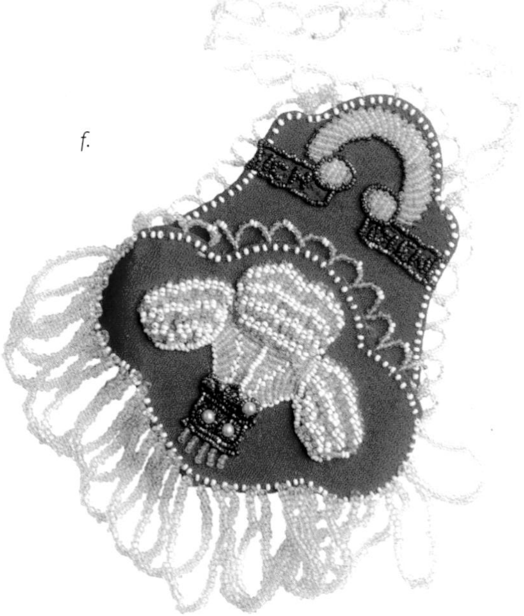

f.

g.

CHAPTER TWO PURSES FROM AROUND THE WORLD

Styles and techniques used in the production of purses in the West have changed through time. This makes it simple to date a sweet purse, for example, to the 17th century, while any collector will know that a pineapple-shaped purse will have been made in the 1820s. In the case of many 19th-century purses, dating can be precisely linked to the publication of the particular women's magazine that included the detailed instructions for its production. In the West, dating a piece is thus important to its identification.

In many other areas of the world, traditional techniques and specific stitches have been passed down through generations of craftsmen and women, making identification by country, region or culture relatively easy. Dating a piece in these instances, however, is more difficult unless aniline dyes have been used. These appeared in the West in the 1850s and spread eastwards through trade thereafter, sometimes replacing vegetable dyes. With the rise in the tourist market, less time-consuming versions of older heirlooms are produced from fabrics and threads coloured with chemical dyes. At the same time, the old heirlooms, with their wealth of exquisite work, may be sold for the trappings of modern life.

Tiny bundles of threads have been wrapped and stitched with beads along the base and up the sides of a tobacco purse. They are strung together with coloured thread.

TURKISH PURSE
This cylindrical purse from Turkey is missing its drawstring, although two holes near the top suggest its one-time existence. Made with blue cotton fabric, the purse is embroidered with repeated motifs in a diaper pattern with laid metal threads and tamboured coloured silks in red, green and pink. A central panel is outlined with a scroll arrangement stitched over cord. The base is also beautifully embroidered. (Embroiderers' Guild)

a.

b.

c.

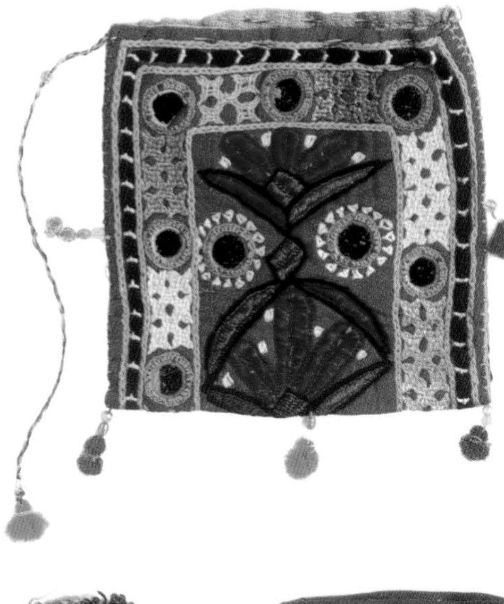
d.

e.

f.

Purses from Asia

a. *SHISHA PURSE*
Exuberantly coloured threads and tassels decorate this purse made recently in the Kutch. Shisha work and counted-thread embroidery, worked on coarse cotton fabric, cover the entire surface. The triangular shapes at each side are formed from diagonally folded squares and are attached to the main part of the purse with insertion stitches. This tobacco purse may have been part of a dowry.

b. *TOBACCO POUCH*
This tobacco pouch, with its distinctive shape, is from Pakistan. The chemically dyed thread indicates that this pouch is relatively modern, but it has been reassembled from a textile made for another purpose. The tassels are tied together and are made from a variety of threads, including silk, cotton and bundles of wool. The charming birds, flowers and leaves are surface-stitched, with some shisha work.

c. *PURSE FROM RAJASTHAN*
In this purse, all the work has been concentrated on the elaborate decoration, with the construction left as simple as possible. The richly embroidered cotton surface of the purse includes open chain, satin stitch and shisha work. In places where the stitches have worn away, the initial workings of the shisha can be seen. Short, tufted tassels are dotted over the surface. The construction could not be simpler: three corners of the finished, embroidered square are folded in and joined with insertion stitching and the fourth corner acts as a flap. Similar purses were made to enclose copies of the Koran.

d. *DRAWSTRING PURSE*
This purse, also from Rajasthan, has a simple construction. Made from a strip of unlined cotton, it is folded in half and the sides joined with insertion stitches. The embroidery includes shisha work, interlacing stitch, stem stitch and couching. The tassels are tiny, bound bundles of brightly coloured wool with beads. A twisted cord is stitched along the top edge and serves both as a drawstring and as a simple handle.

e. *FOLDING AFGHAN PURSE*
A continuous, lined strip of embroidered cotton forms the back of this purse from Afghanistan. Two further squares, similarly embroidered with designs in chain stitch and shisha work, have been seamed to form two pockets. The embroidery is in cotton and metallic threads, some of which have become worn with use. The seams are covered with orange and green beads. The whole piece is folded twice to form a pocketed purse. Two press studs on the corners of a flap close the purse.

f. *TURKISH PURSE*
This Turkish purse, with its characteristic outlined floral motif, was allegedly made to contain a gift of money on the occasion of a boy's circumcision. The red lining extends above the thin cream fabric and is doubled over to form a channel for the drawstring cord. Leaf sprigs and a single flower motif are outlined in couched gold thread and cord. The leaves and flower are filled in with straight stitches and single chain stitches in red thread.

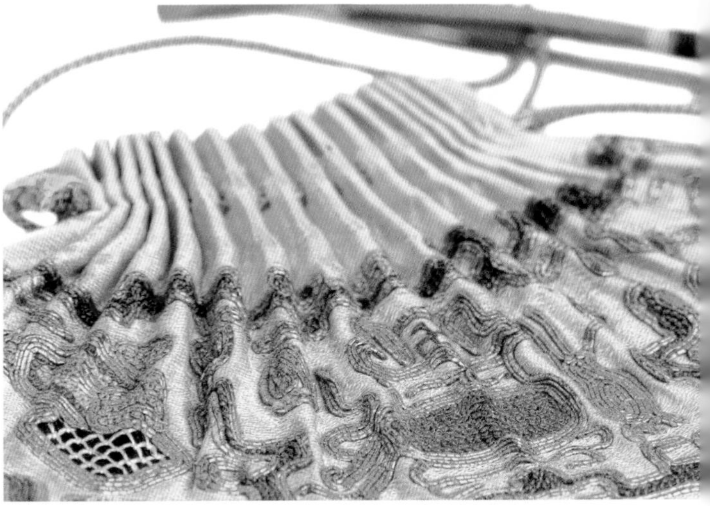

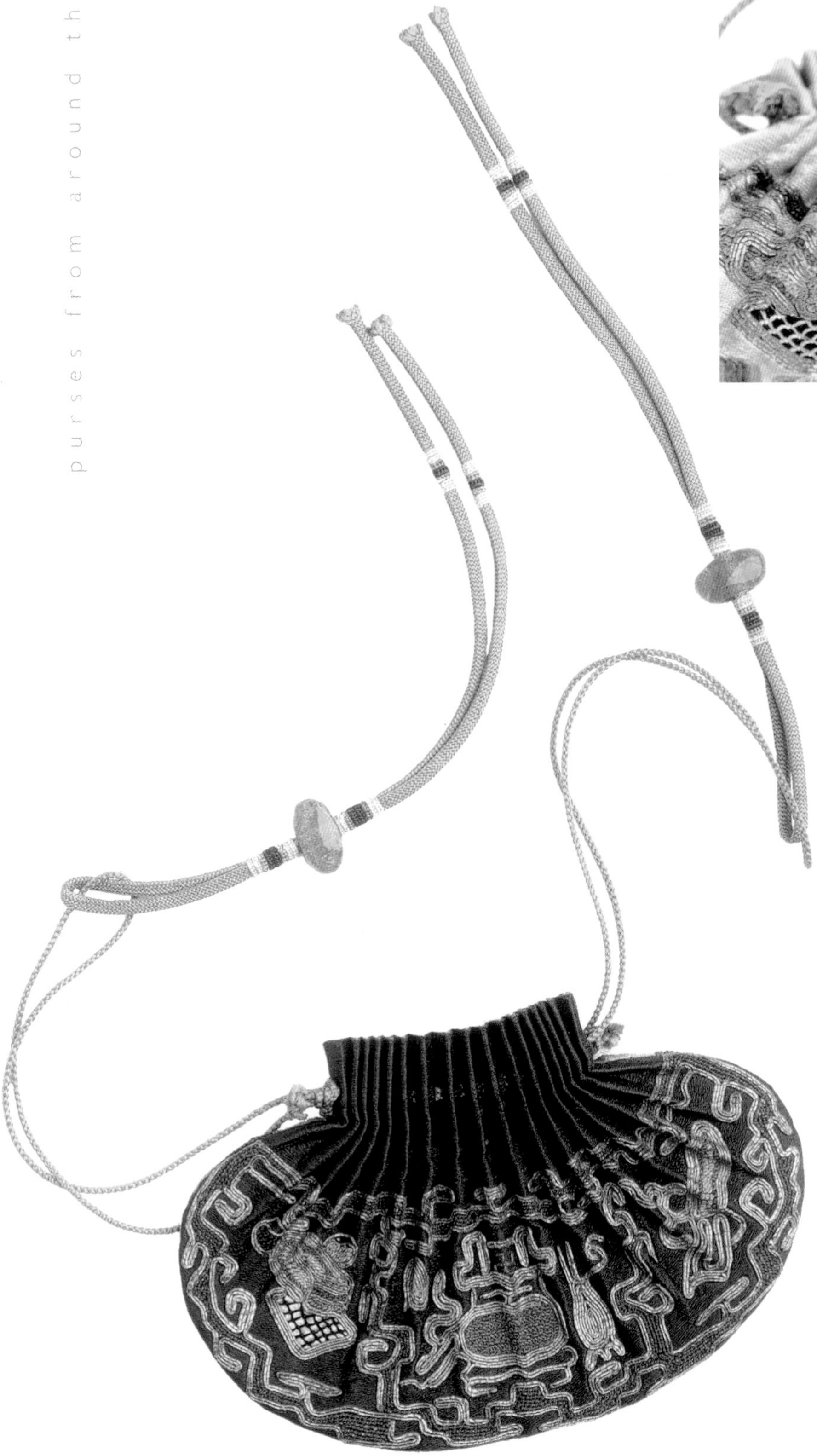

Purses from China

INCENSE PURSE FROM CHINA
(front and back)
Incense purses were used by both men and women in China and were hung around the waist or from a lapel. Other items, such as fan cases and tobacco pouches, were also strung from the belt. A small piece of cotton wadding impregnated with aromatic herbs or incense was placed inside, to be used like cologne. When opened out, this purse is a large pocket shape. The sharp pleating is achieved with a lining of paper, stiffened with rice paste. The two sides are embroidered in Peking knots, couched gold threads and other laid work. The embroidery is identical on both sides but is worked on ground fabrics of different colours and the two sides consequently look very different. The drawstring passes directly through holes made in the pleats and has beaded and bound braids looped through at each side.

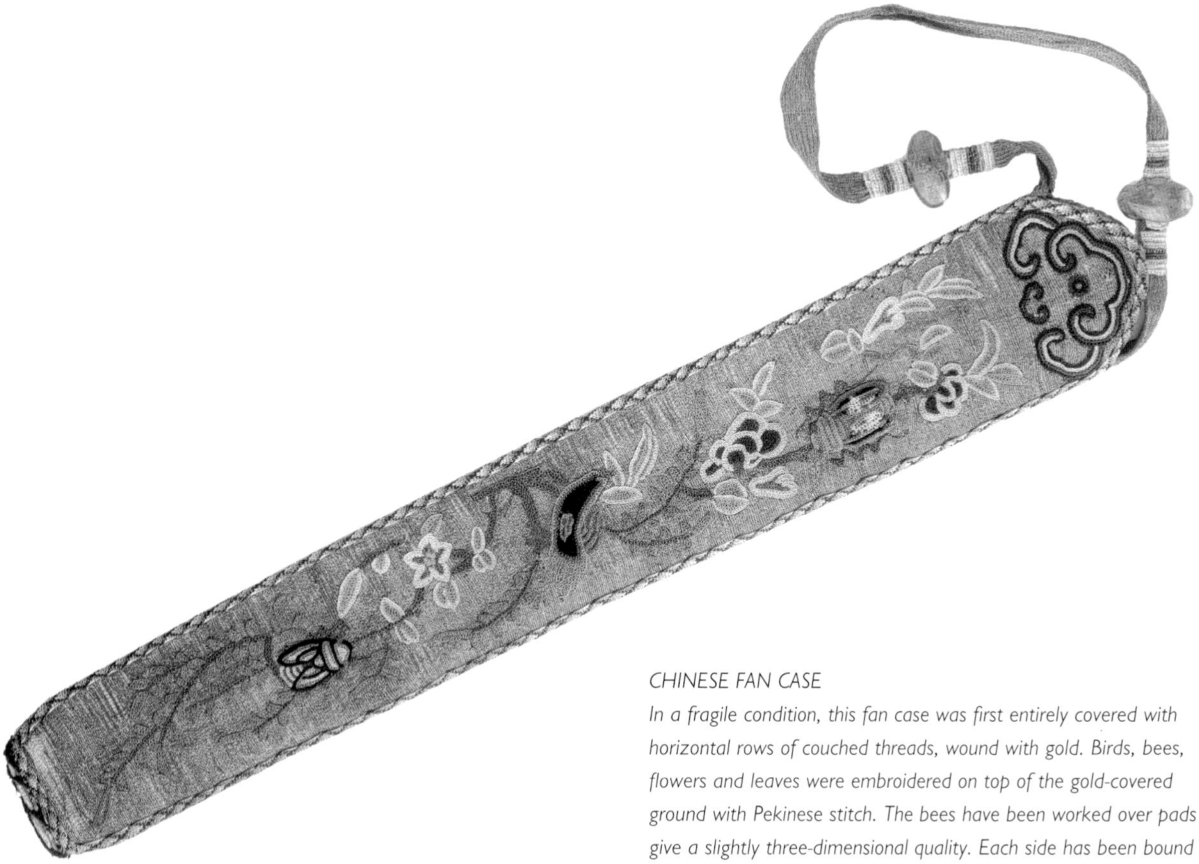

CHINESE FAN CASE
In a fragile condition, this fan case was first entirely covered with horizontal rows of couched threads, wound with gold. Birds, bees, flowers and leaves were embroidered on top of the gold-covered ground with Pekinese stitch. The bees have been worked over pads to give a slightly three-dimensional quality. Each side has been bound with braid and stitched together down the sides. A small oval base adds a little more room for a fan and a typical woven handle with beads and wrapped cords has been attached to the top corners.

CYLINDRICAL CHINESE PURSE
Measuring 13cm (5in) long, this purse consists of two fabric cylinders, one fitting inside the other. The outer cylinder is exquisitely embroidered with gold-covered thread and coloured silks in Pekinese stitch and seed stitch. The ground fabric is dark blue silk and is in a fragile state.

CHAPTER THREE GETTING STARTED

If a purse is to be created as an accessory for use at a special occasion and with a particular outfit, there will be certain restrictions as to its size and shape. Considerations include whether the purse should contrast with, or complement the outfit; how big it should be in relation to the height of the user, what it must hold and whether it should be a handbag, shoulder or clutch bag.

The purses in this book are mostly designed as precious items of exquisite workmanship and not as handbags for everyday use. Some may be used as evening purses for special occasions, perhaps as 'showstoppers', in complete contrast to a plain outfit. Most will be decorative items, exquisite in themselves, and beautifully crafted works of art. Some may be created to enclose precious gift items, others as gifts themselves, to be displayed among treasured possessions. These will be made as one-off pieces, personal to the maker. In this case, there need be no restrictions as to shape, decoration or embellishments. The choice of materials is boundless and the design possibilities are infinite.

Another important consideration is the reason for making the purse. It could be that you have been excited by particular colours, shapes or embellishments. Alternatively, it may be that you have been deeply touched by something and wish to use the creation of a purse as a vehicle to express your idea. Perhaps you want to convey a sense of a place, or a memory of a particular event, or you wish to commemorate a special occasion. Alternatively, it could be that the purse is to be a special, and appropriate, 'gift wrapping' for an exceptional present.

HORSE-CHESTNUT PURSE
Made as a 'showstopper', Emily Jo Gibbs's beautifully crafted horse-chestnut purse is at once organic and witty. The whole hand-crafted piece, with its novel source of inspiration and meticulous attention to detail, is both immensely pleasing and humorous.

Purses as containers

One of the obvious reasons for making a purse is to use it as a container. Containment is part of the nature of a purse, and there is an element of secrecy about the insides of purses. If a purse is used as an accessory, there is an understanding of the sanctity of the contents, so that delving into someone else's purse is considered a violation. In a slightly different way, purses made as 'showstoppers' may contain secreted objects, which only add to the mystery, providing an additional surprise.

The following three inspirational purses have been created with enclosed objects that in each case form an integral part of the design.

MAUREEN KING'S WALNUT PURSE

Maureen King's walnut-shell purse is a modern interpretation of the 17th-century novelty purse. Two walnut shells were first covered with velvet and padded and lined with silk. Each side was then embroidered with couched gold thread and seed pearls. Twisted gold threads and silk cords, some knotted and beaded with unbelievably small beads, form the tassel, which is 19cm (7½in) long. The handles and fastening are made with plaited gold tambour threads. Inside the shell is a 'walnut', 2.5cm (1in) across, which is covered in metal threads worked in random chain stitch and tiny pearls. Even the nut is hinged and lined with silk.

HORSE-CHESTNUT PURSE

The shape of this purse by Emily Jo Gibbs was created with two hinged rings, each of which supports a silk and satin dome. It is exquisitely made, each half consisting of six triangular pieces of silk dupion, stitched to form a cup shape, with a similarly constructed six-panelled duchesse satin lining. Thirty silk spikes are attached, their tips wound with copper wire. Inside, a six-panelled satin conker nestles, appropriately brown and shiny. A wire hook-and-eye clasp and a wire-bound handle complete the purse. *For a closer look, see page 24.*

EMILY JO GIBBS'S FACE PURSE

Emily has also fashioned a 'Face Purse', designed as one of a group of three, and based on Russian dolls that fit inside one another. The spherical shape is created with blocking net, generally used to make hats. This has been covered with painted silk, and brass 'curls' have been couched to the surface to represent the hair. The features are couched metal shapes, and the whole has a silver gilt frame, made by Emily.

Inspirations

Being faced with a blank canvas and the burning desire to make a purse can be daunting. It can also be exciting – the beginning of a creative journey. Part of any new adventure in designing a textile piece is to start by gathering information. For this, there is nothing more inspiring than a new sketchbook or scrap book in which to accumulate all the relevant ideas. Your initial reasons for wanting to make a purse must go in, whether it is the wish to convey a memory, or because you would like to commemorate a special occasion, or that you have been inspired to make a special container for a gift. This can take the form of words, but could also be conveyed in collages, drawings, cuttings, painted papers or photographs.

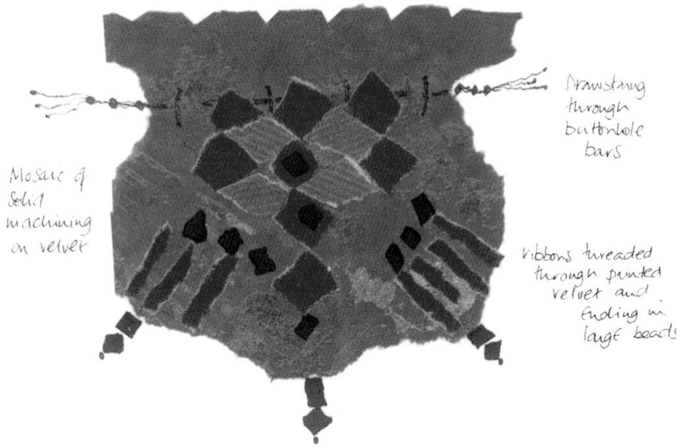

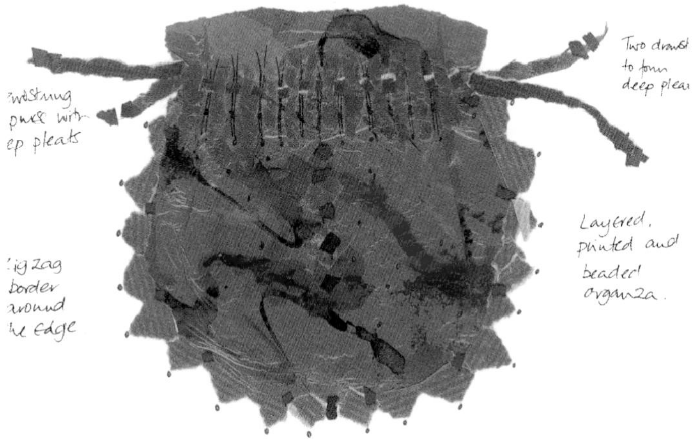

Torn and cut decorated papers can be used to explore ideas. Make notes of possible interpretations in fabrics and threads alongside your work.

The shape

Having decided what the purse is to be for and having noted your initial reasons for making one, it is often tempting to plunge straight into thinking about the decoration, but it is better to start with the shape. Interesting shapes for purses can be seen all around us. Initial inspiration for the shape of your purse may come from such diverse sources as pieces of jewellery, architectural features or details of ornamental artefacts.

Photographs and cuttings from magazines can be of enormous value. Thumbnail sketches of interesting outlines of objects can be inspirational in themselves. Sometimes a photograph or drawing, turned upside down, suggests unexpected shapes for purses. When you start to look, it is possible to see potential shapes all around you. It is well worth spending some time gathering potential shapes at this stage, because in so doing, your eye will be trained to notice more and more design opportunities, and the larger your collection of shapes, the more appropriate the selection will be.

A few simple collages of torn papers can be enormously inspiring. Tissue papers are particularly good to use as they can be pleated and shaped with ease. They will look all the better if they have been personalized in some way, perhaps by painting inks on them or by printing random patterns in paint.

The shape of your purse will give some idea as to whether it should be flat or more three-dimensional, with a gusset or with several sides. The shape you choose may also give some indication as to whether your purse will have a top fastening or a flap, and where there are opportunities for fasteners and attachment of handles.

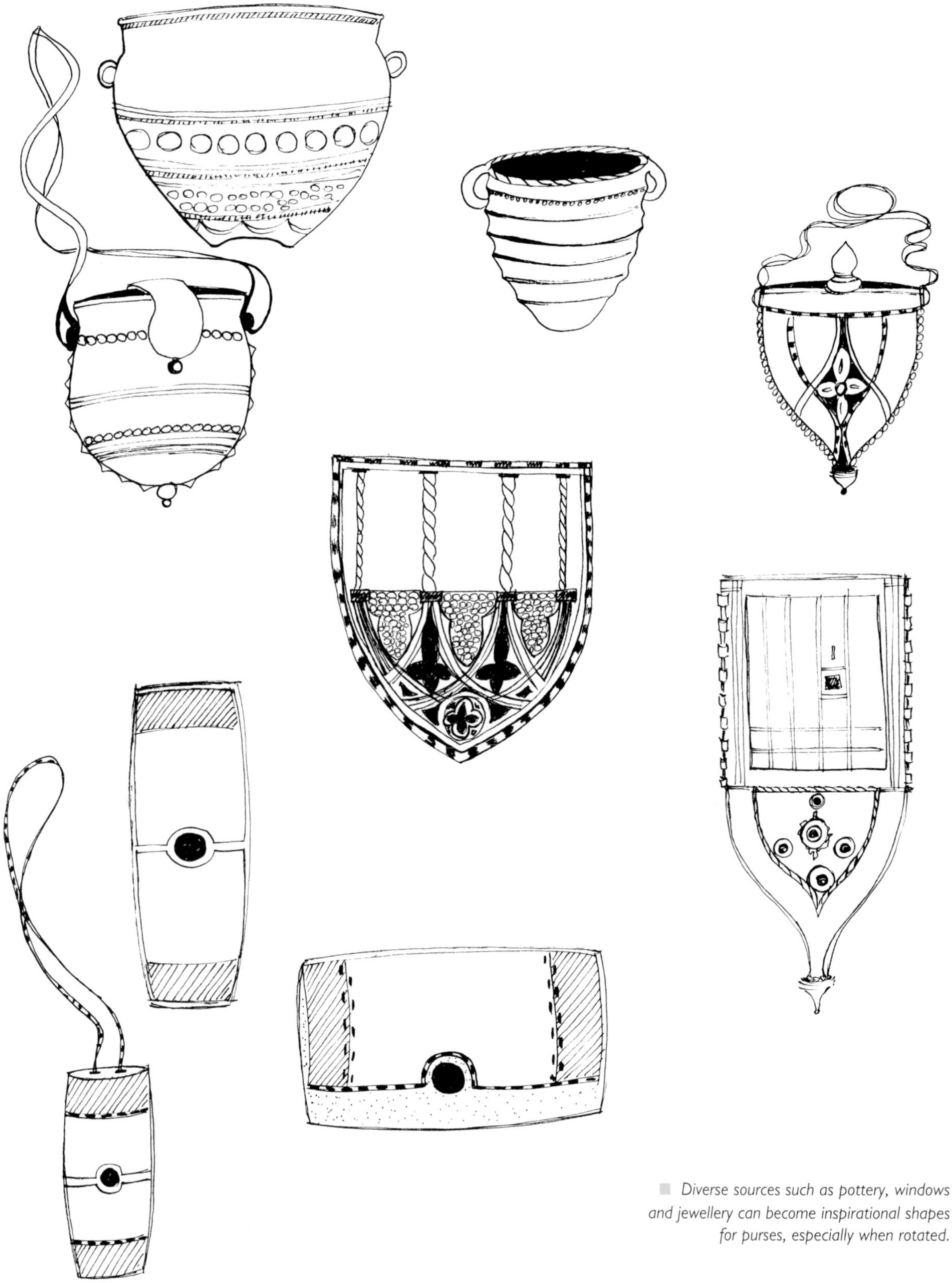

Diverse sources such as pottery, windows and jewellery can become inspirational shapes for purses, especially when rotated.

Paper mock-ups

Having chosen your shape, try out possible purses in paper first, in the same way that a dressmaker makes a toile before making the final dress. Enlarge the paper shapes to the required size using a photocopier, making several copies, and stick them together using masking tape. Use string to make handles. By making a mock-up you can also gauge the correct size for the opening, check whether the interior is accessible, and determine the size and design of the fastening. See page 42.

Paper patterns

When these problems are solved, adjust the other photocopies to match the design. Add seam allowances, if they are required. Glue the copies to thin card and cut out. These are your templates or patterns. It is a good idea to write on the templates the name of the purse, the part (front, back, gusset and so on), how many pieces are needed, and indications of any seam allowances. All the templates for a purse can be stored in a labelled envelope or plastic folder for easy future reference.

Materials

Purses can be made from practically any material. Throughout the world, purses have been made from a vast selection of resources: sealskin, fish skin, fish scales and beetles' wings, beads, shells and bark – it seems anything can be used. As can be seen in the purses shown below and opposite, the choice of materials is extremely wide and can even be bizarre. In short, any material that is considered with care and used appropriately can be employed. For this reason, it is a good idea to pin or clip possible materials into your sketchbook.

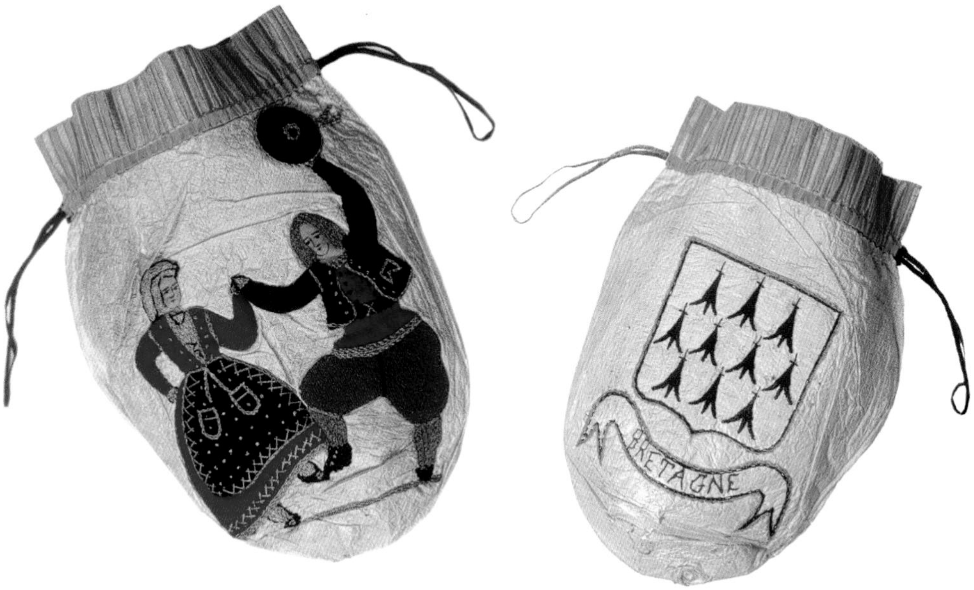

A PURSE FROM BRITTANY

This purse is made from the most unpromising of materials, probably in the 19th century. A design of two dancing figures in traditional dress is worked in wool fabrics applied to a pig's bladder. The figures are embroidered with silk threads in chain stitch and the faces are painted on silk fabric. The purse is lined with a striped silk fabric and finished with a wide ribbon above a drawstring channel. The shield motif on the reverse, with the word 'Bretagne' emblazoned below, suggests that it may have been made as a commemorative piece. It measures 18 x 13cm (7 x 5in). (Embroiderers' Guild)

RECYCLED NUMBER-PLATE PURSE

This American purse was created from recycled materials by a company called Littlearth. Although not embroidered, it has been designed, constructed and embellished with a great deal of thought. American car number plates have been expertly riveted together to make a cylinder, the ends of which are reused hub-caps. A hinged flap makes an opening, which can be closed with a press-stud on a leather tab, decorated with a bottle-top. It is imaginatively finished with a handle made from an inner tube.

Using colour

Colour is all around us. We are overwhelmed with colour and yet it is often difficult to choose colours for specific purposes. It is a good idea to note down colours that attract you by collecting pictures from magazines or postcards of favourite paintings. Gorgeous colour combinations can be seen in gardens – newly emerging leaves, brick walls or stone paths, for example – and in man-made decorative objects, including paintings; in fact anywhere. Record those that attract you using photography, torn scraps from colour magazines, aquarelle pencils, watercolours or oil pastels (see opposite page). Fill in small blocks of colour in the proportions in which they occur in your source. Try to replicate the colours as exactly as you can. A window template of your purse shape could be moved across sketchbook pages of solid colours or magazine pages as an aid to considering their arrangement on the purse (see page 36).

Another way of choosing colour combinations is to make swatches of possible materials for your purse (below). Cut and pile up small pieces of fabrics, ribbons and bindings, together with possible threads and beads, in roughly the proportions they may be used on a purse. Arrange and rearrange these until you arrive at a combination you find pleasing. These could be pinned into your sketchbook for future reference.

It is important to make sure that there is contrast in the colours, tones or textures of the fabrics used. Contrast in one of these elements will make a more arresting design. While choice of colour is personal, it is nevertheless well known that an unexpected element in a design will make it more interesting. This could be a daring colour combination, unusual textures together, or an extra-large bead used as a fastening. All these could make the difference between a purse that is ordinary and one that has an immediate and recognizable appeal.

Plain and patterned silks and velvets, arranged in pleasing combinations with beads, braids and ribbons, can give an idea of how the colours and fabrics might look in the finished purse.

Opposite page ■ A sketchbook page showing a stylized painting of a garden. Acrylic paints and large brushes were used to convey the contrasting patches of light and deep shadows.

Decoration

Sometimes the shape of the purse will suggest ideas for the arrangement of the embellishments; collages, as previously described in the section about shape, could also help. There are decisions to be made about the nature of the decoration and where on the purse it will occur. Will the purse be highly decorative or restrained in its appearance, and will it have a repeat pattern of decoration, an all-over arrangement, a central motif or an asymmetrical, unexpected arrangement? It is a good idea to try out several arrangements of embellishments on copies of the overall shape.

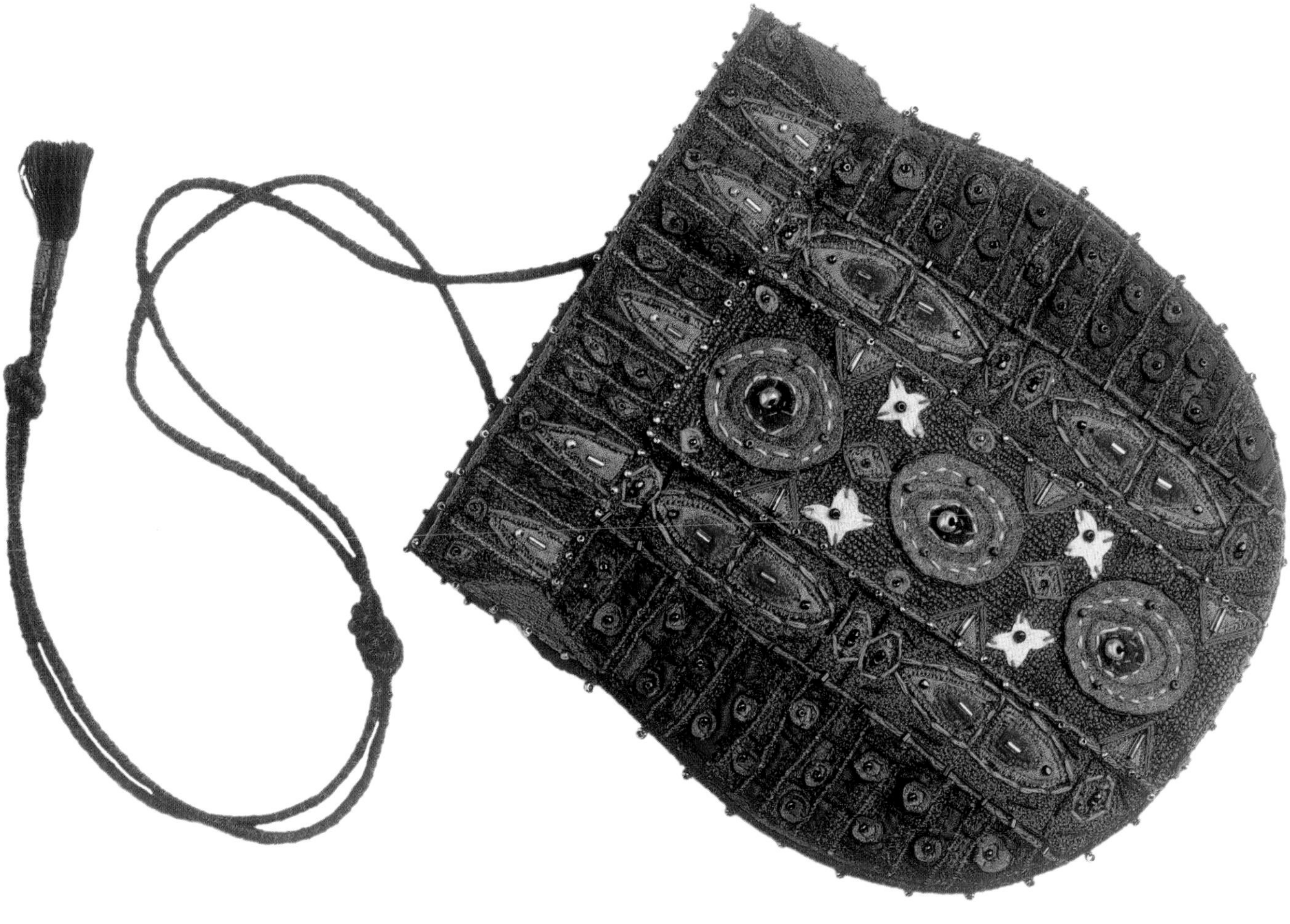

HILARY BOWER'S PURSE

Hilary Bower's purse, made in the 1990s and measuring 19cm (7½in) wide and 21cm (8¼in) long, is a celebration of the decorated surface. Cotton fabric, layered with silk organza and heavily machine stitched in a variety of patterns, is further embellished with small pieces of velvet, leather, felt, beads and hand-stitching. Lined with silk and with a machined-cord tassel, the subtle colours of this purse are accentuated with small turquoise stitches. The decoration is different on each side. Hilary no longer makes purses but over the last decade has developed her concepts of containment and enclosure further and now creates wall-hung vessels with the same attention to detail.

One method of experimenting with decoration is to cut out a window template of your purse shape and move this over sketchbook pages or even over magazine pages to get ideas for unusual arrangements (see diagram below). To do this, cut out the shape of your purse in stiff paper or thin card; place this in the centre of a piece of paper, draw round the shape and cut it out, leaving a 'window' outline of your purse. Move this window over your page of decoration, turning the window as you go. The window will allow you to isolate an attractive arrangement for decoration within the purse outline. Trace the outlines of your purse and the decoration and pin this in your sketchbook. Try several possibilities. It may be that one looks right; if this is the case, then it could be developed as the plan for your purse.

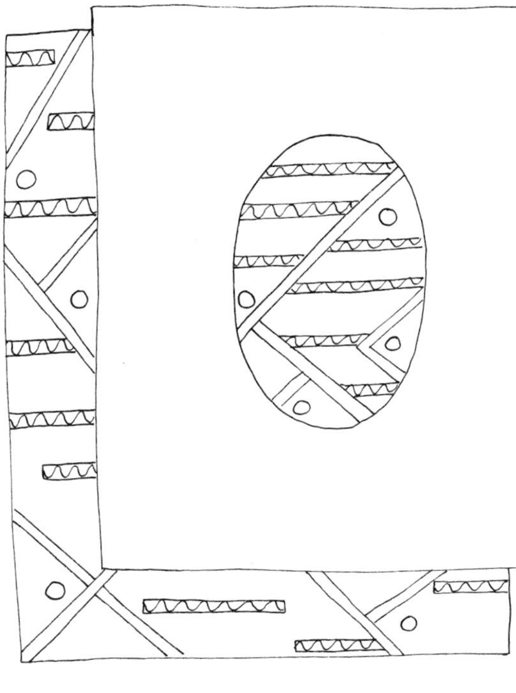

Unexpected arrangements of decoration on a purse can be achieved using a window template.

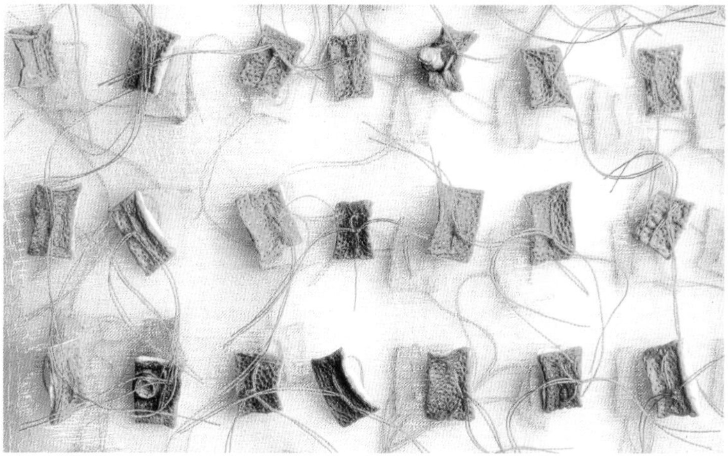

A grid pattern of cut and dried lemon peel is stitched on organza. Cotton threads are left haphazardly loose and the lemon peel is attractively wayward, creating a lively surface.

Equipment

With some knowledge of basic dressmaking techniques, it is possible to construct an attractive and unusual purse. Skills such as binding edges, hemming and seaming both straight and curved edges will all be extremely useful.

- The usual needlework equipment, including a very sharp pair of embroidery scissors, sharp fabric scissors, pins, a selection of sewing and embroidery needles, a thimble and some sewing threads, are all essential.
- Many purses can be made by hand, but a sewing machine will make certain processes faster and seaming stronger. In some instances, it is useful to have a zigzag oversewing facility on the machine, but a straight stitch is usually all that is needed.
- Keep a selection of fabrics and embroidery threads, ribbons, beads and braids. I never throw any of these out on the premise that the larger the collection, the better the chance of being able to select the exactly appropriate piece. Silk, organza, linen and cotton fabrics, either plain or patterned and commercially produced or hand-dyed, can all be used.
- A sliver remaining from a bar of soap is useful for marking dark fabrics. The edge can be sharpened with a craft knife and you will find that the mark on the fabric gradually wears off during stitching. An added bonus is that the fabric may even smell fragrant while it is being worked. To mark lighter fabrics, use a commercial fabric pen.
- Pelmet Vilene (Pellon) can be used to stiffen fabrics. It is available from curtaining shops in various weights and widths. The weight you use will depend on the fabric to be backed. Sheer fabrics may need a sandwich layer of additional wadding in order to overcome hard edges.
- Bondaweb (Wonder-Under), available from haberdashers' shops, is a fusible, paper-backed tissue that is used to bond two fabrics together.
- It is also useful to have a cutting board and a craft knife, paper cutting scissors and a rotary cutter.

Design and finish

Whatever the nature of the purse, attention to detail and finish is of paramount importance. A beautifully designed purse would be marred by poor workmanship. Equally, an exquisitely worked and finished purse of poor design will be a disappointment. So good design and perfect finish are both essential.

Purses can be as complicated or as simple as the maker chooses. They need not be fiendishly difficult to make and indeed some of the simplest purses are the most successful. But if 'elaborate' is what is required, then a purse can be a *tour de force* – a fantastic apprentice piece or a work of art.

CHAPTER FOUR SIMPLE TWO-SIDED PURSES

For the beginner, the simplest starting point is perhaps the two-sided purse. The method outlined in this chapter can be used to make many different versions.

In the previous chapter the basic considerations were outlined. Shape, use, patterns and mock-ups, materials, colour and decoration were discussed. We now come to putting these considerations into practice and making specific purses, using the entire process from inspiration to completion.

In the following chapters there are several sets of instructions for making purses. These are intended to be core methods. They can all be adapted to create personalized purses using one's own design sources, shapes, colours and embellishments, as described in Chapter Three.

For the beginner, the simplest starting point is perhaps the two-sided purse, which can be adapted to make a whole series of similarly constructed, but very different purses.

Paper models can be used to experiment with shape. When making a symmetrical purse such as the one shown opposite, it is always better to cut the shape out of paper folded in half vertically, thus ensuring the symmetry.

In a relatively simple purse attention to detail, bindings and fastenings can add interest, as can contrasting empty and busy areas on the surface.

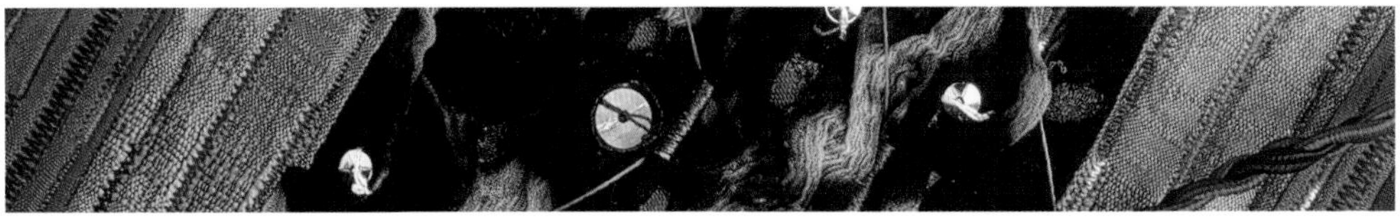

Detail of an oblong two-sided purse made with bleached and machine embroidered organza and dupion silk borders.

A PURSE BASED ON A CHINESE SCENT BOTTLE
A strip of patchwork, black and white fabrics and matching braid and beads combine to make this striking two-sided purse. See page 43 for instructions on making this purse.

A purse inspired by a Chinese scent bottle

A Chinese scent bottle was the inspiration for the purse shown on page 38. First, the scent bottle was drawn and the outline shape reproduced several times using a photocopier. The shape could also be copied by tracing. Several possible designs were tried out in black and white (see opposite). A variety of ways of dividing up the space was tried, and Chinese motifs were experimentally used in some of these. By initially working in black and white, the form and composition of the shape of a purse and its decoration is emphasized and it is easier to avoid being seduced by colour at an early stage. Proportions of busy and empty areas can be seen and considered more easily.

Once the shape and arrangement of embellishments have been worked out, several colourways could be considered. The colour could have been taken from the delicate colours of the original bottle or they could have been inspired by colour studies of leaves, paintings or any of the colour sources suggested in the last chapter. But for the purposes of this first purse, black and white were chosen. Indeed it may be that in many cases a black-and-white arrangement will suit the requirements very well, or that a black-and-white purse with a single stunning turquoise bead is just perfect for a particular occasion.

Beautiful man-made objects are a constant source of inspiration. A Chinese scent bottle, painstakingly painted on the inside of frosted glass, was the inspiration for a simple two-sided purse.

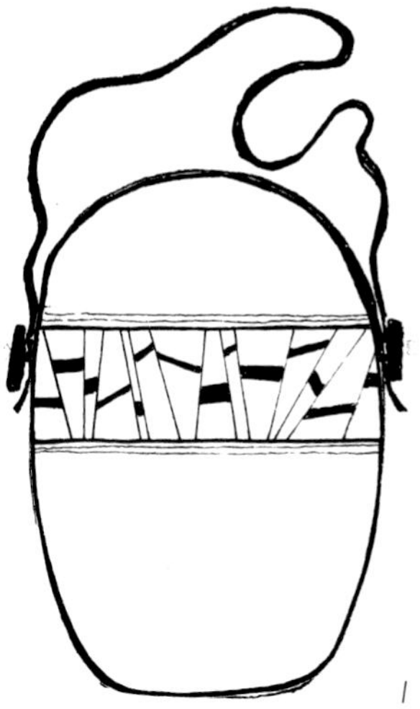

1

2

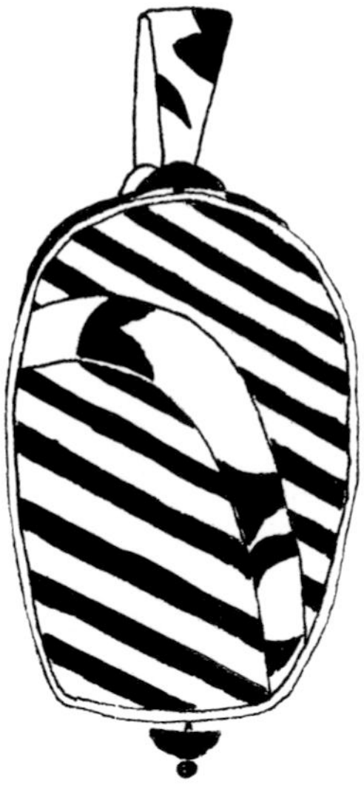

3

PURSE DESIGNS

1 Instructions for this patched purse are given on page 43.

2 Two pieced halves are seamed diagonally to create a counterchange effect here.

3 Using curved seams, striped fabric is combined with floral fabric, which is also used for the shaped handle.

4 A plain front is embroidered in curved lines.

5 Contrasting coloured fabric strips are bonded to the front of this purse and are echoed in the choice of beads.

6 Hand-embroidered discs appear to float across the surface of the front of this purse. The fastening is also circular (see Fastenings, page 122). A painted wooden bar is passed through the two bound circles in the back.

7 Couched lines of embroidery threads, white on black and black on white, form the simple decoration for this purse.

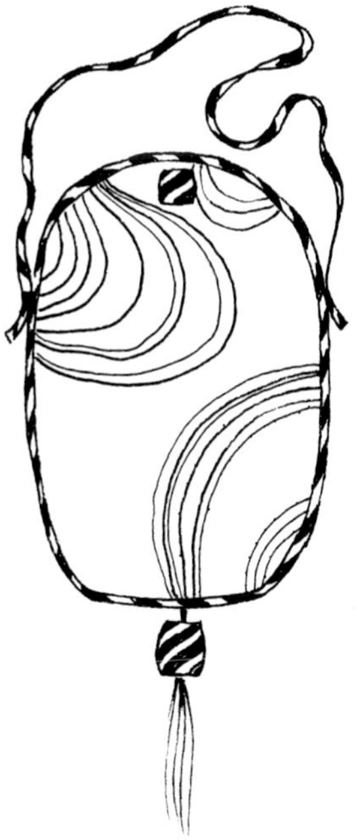

4

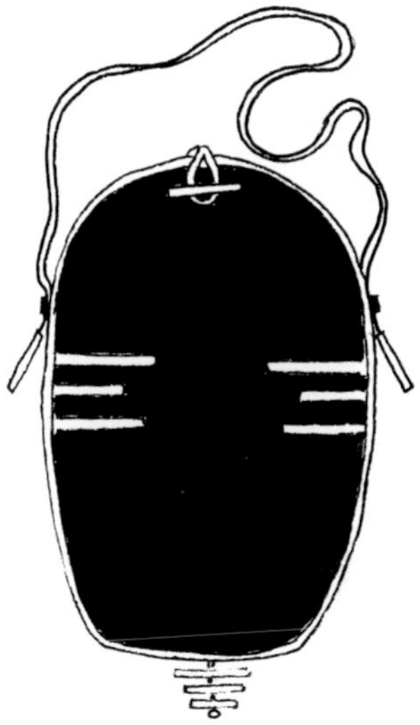

5

6

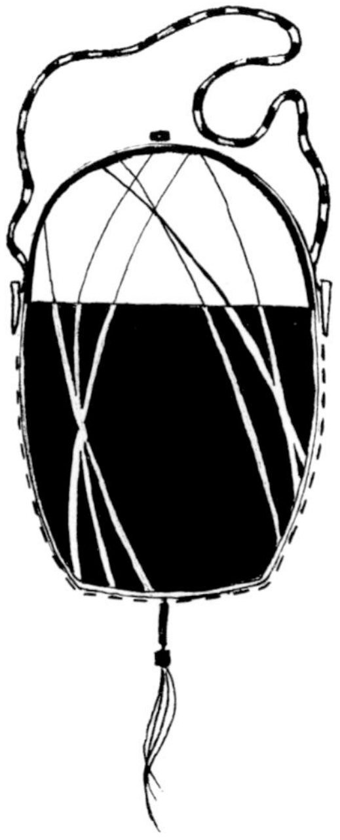

7

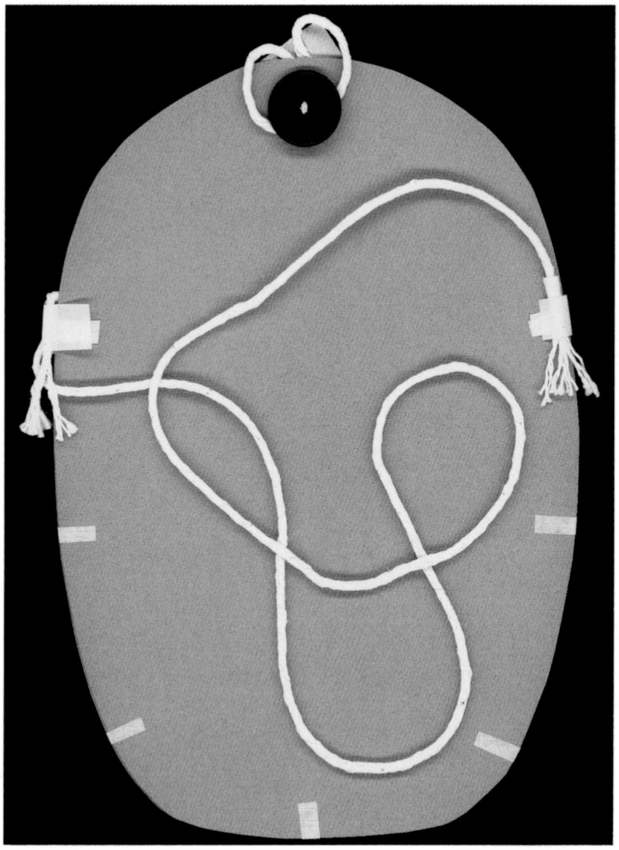

Paper mock-up of
the simple two-sided purse.

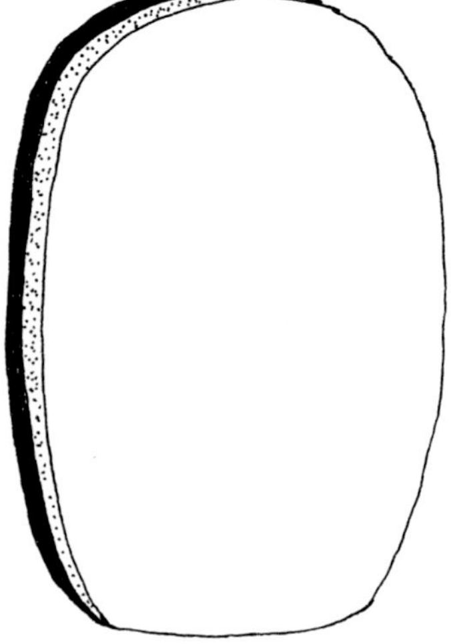

Diagram 1

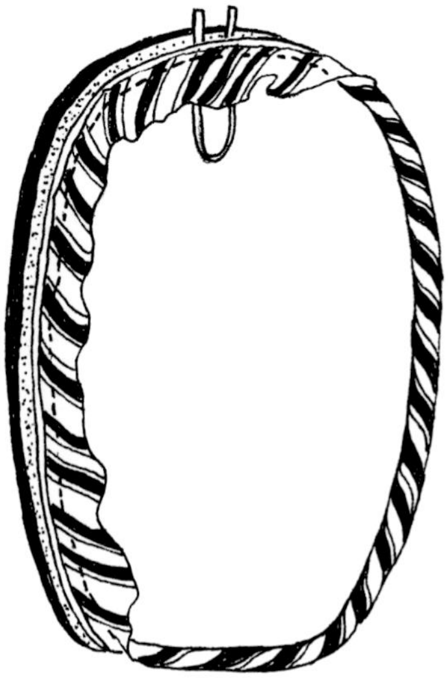

Diagram 2

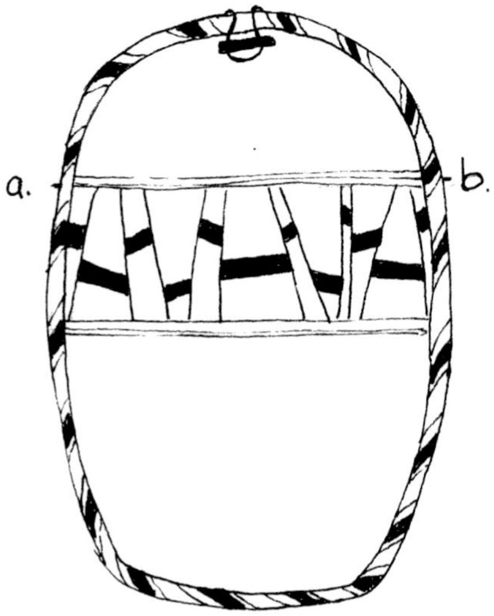

Diagram 3

HOW TO MAKE A TWO-SIDED PURSE

Start by making a paper mock-up, as shown opposite. Make four full-size copies of the purse shape. The first two, one the front and the other the back, can be held together with small strips of masking tape. I decided to place the handle attachments about a third of the way around the edge, as this was aesthetically pleasing and allowed easy access to the interior. Then I determined the size of the fastening and the length of the cord to go round it. On this purse, no seam allowances are needed as the edges are bound. The other two photocopies can be stuck to thin card, labelled and cut out, and used as the pattern.

Materials

For the purse:

- 30 x 40cm (12 x 16in) thin card
- 30 x 40cm (12 x 16in) pelmet Vilene (Pellon)
- 30 x 40cm (12 x 16in) lining fabric
- 30 x 20cm (12 x 8in) fabric for back of purse (black)
- 30 x 20cm (12 x 8in) fabric for front of purse (white)
- 150cm (60in) length crossways-cut strip, 3cm (1¼in) wide, for binding (see page 103)

For the Seminole patchwork:

- 2 pieces white fabric, each 20 x 30cm (8 x 12in)
- 1 strip black fabric, 30 x 3cm (12 x 1¼ in)

Method

1. Using thin card, make a pattern to the size you require, adjusting fabric requirements if you make your purse larger or smaller than the one illustrated. The purse shown here is 24cm (9½in) long by 17cm (6½in) wide. Use this template to cut a piece of pelmet Vilene and one of lining fabric and, using Bondaweb, bond them together (see diagram 1). Now bond a piece of the fabric intended for the back of the purse to the other side of the pelmet Vilene (Pellon), and bind it with crossways-cut fabric, incorporating a loop of cord or ribbon as shown in diagram 2. The loop must be long enough to go over the bound edge and around a bead or button stitched to the front of the purse. That completes the back.

2. Using the pattern, make the front by cutting a piece each of pelmet Vilene (Pellon) and lining fabric and bonding them together as for the back. Make a strip of Seminole patchwork as described on page 119, using black and white cottons or silks. Trim away the excess fabric to make a strip 8cm (3¼in) deep and as wide as the purse front. Seam white fabric to the top and bottom of the strip; press the seams and machine a few horizontal lines in black, stitching each side of the patchwork panel. Bond the front lining to the back of the patchwork, making sure the patchwork is straight, horizontally. Trim around the perimeter. Bind the front in the same way as the back of the purse but omit the card loop. Pin front and back together and oversew the edge from *a* to *b*, as shown in diagram 3. Stitch an appropriate bead or button to the front of the purse. For the handle, double a length of black-and-white braid and stitch at *a* and *b*, leaving the ends free. Stitch beads at intervals along the handle.

LETTER PURSE
Inspired by the two-sided letter purses displayed in the Indian Gallery of the Victoria and Albert Museum, London, this purse has a central panel surrounded by borders. Randomly bleached organza was gathered and stitched down with zigzag machining and hand-stitched sequins. Small holes were burnt with a soldering iron and the central panel lined with red silk to show through the holes. The borders were added and also stitched with zigzag machining. The two sides were then stitched and bound together. Plaited red-and-black Russia braid cords were stitched to the sides for a handle and a red-and-black painted Chinese bead was added as a fastening.

Variations of the Two-Sided Purse

This method of construction, in which the back and the front of the purse are completed separately before being sewn together, offers many possibilities for experimentation. For example, the overall outline can be changed from an oval to an oblong shape, as for the letter purse shown opposite.

Another idea is to extend the back to form a flap. As can be seen on the following two pages, the shape of the flap can also alter the appearance of the purse.

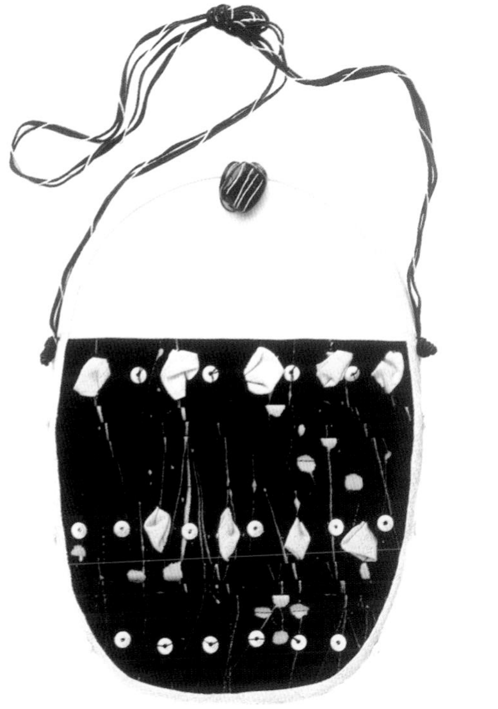

BLEACHED VELVET PURSE
Another version of the basic two-sided purse uses the scratched and whitened lines on the surface of a bead as inspiration. Black cotton velvet was trailed with thick household bleach to achieve similar vertical lines. Bleach can be used on fabrics, provided that they are neutralized by soaking in vinegar afterwards. The bleached velvet was slashed with sharp embroidery scissors and strips of cream-coloured slubbed silk were pulled through the slashes from the back. The silk was then secured at intervals with cream-coloured beads. A cord of doubled Russia braid, wrapped with cream-coloured thread, was knotted at both ends and stitched to the sides. Further beads around the edge complete the purse.

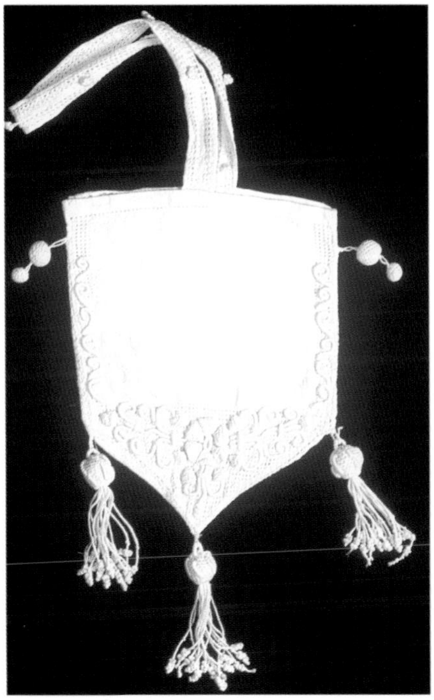

CASAL GUIDI PURSE
There is something very beguiling and aesthetically pleasing about monochromatic pieces, which accentuate textures. This early 20th-century purse, 18cm (7in) wide by 23cm (9in) long, comes from Casal Guidi in Italy. This village near Pistoia gives its name to the embroidery practised there. Linen is stitched with a matching thread in pulled-thread work and a variety of buttonhole stitches. In this purse, the symmetrically arranged floral motif has been worked in detached buttonhole stitch and whipped threads over a ground that has been initially textured with pulled work. The characteristic bobble tassels on the corners are worked in buttonhole stitch over scraps of fabric, the larger lower tassels with knotted cotton threads. The handle is a hemmed linen strip, with pulled work along each edge. (Embroiderers' Guild)

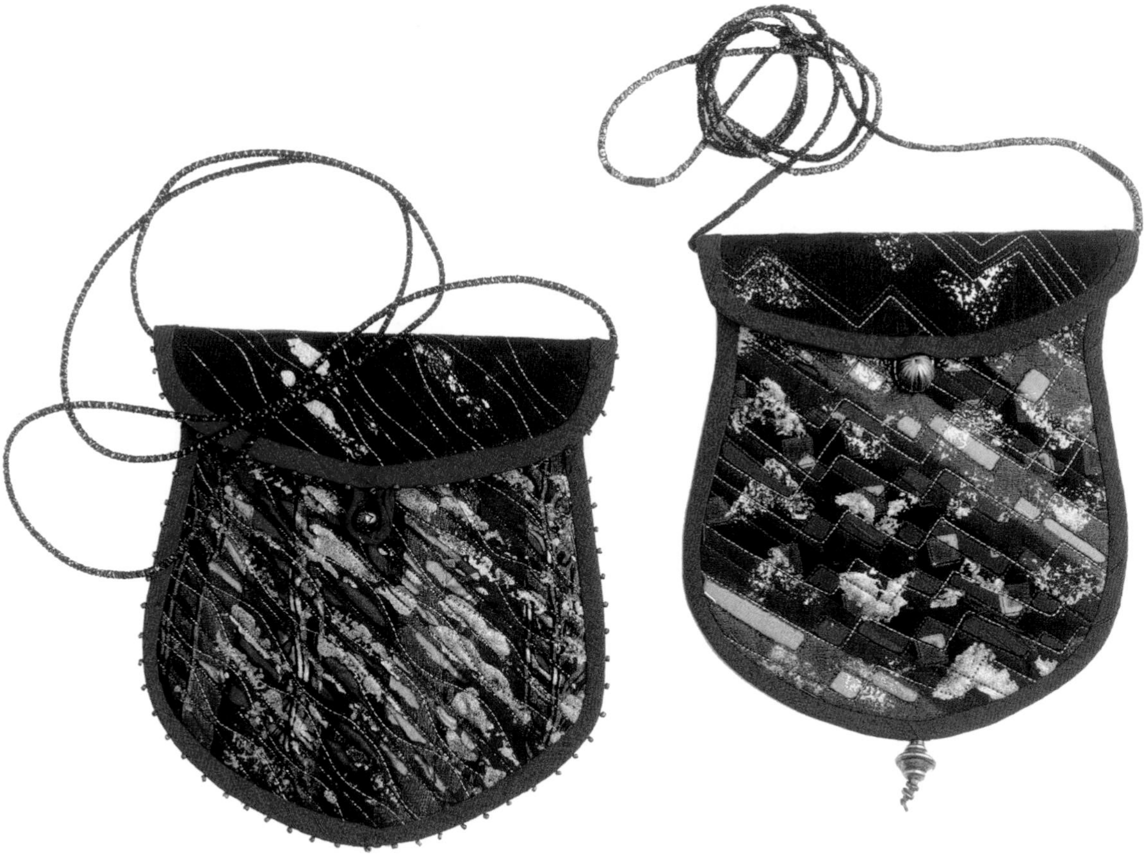

TWO SLASHED PURSES

These two purses were inspired by an example seen in the Rachel Kay-Shuttleworth Collection at Gawthorpe Hall. The front panels were cut out of pelmet Vilene (Pellon) and covered with torn strips of old 1960s Indian silk scarves. Organza was laid over and machine-stitched in place with metallic variegated thread in wavy or stepped lines. The organza was slashed at intervals with a craft knife, and some gold fabric paint was printed over the surface. The fronts were lined and the top edges were bound with a strip of silk. Finally, tiny beads were stitched along the edge of one purse and on the second, a tassel made of several beads strung together provided the finishing touch. The backs were made up with plain black silk stitched with metallic threads and lined. Fronts and backs were stitched together right sides out. The edges of each purse were bound with crossways purple silk running all around and incorporating a small loop on the flap. Handles of machined string (see page 108) were anchored with a small horizontal channel on the inside of the flap. Finally, a small bead was added as a fastening.

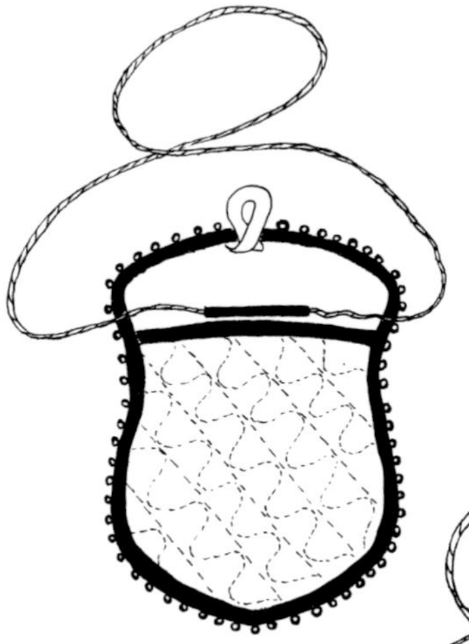

Diagram 1

Diagram 2

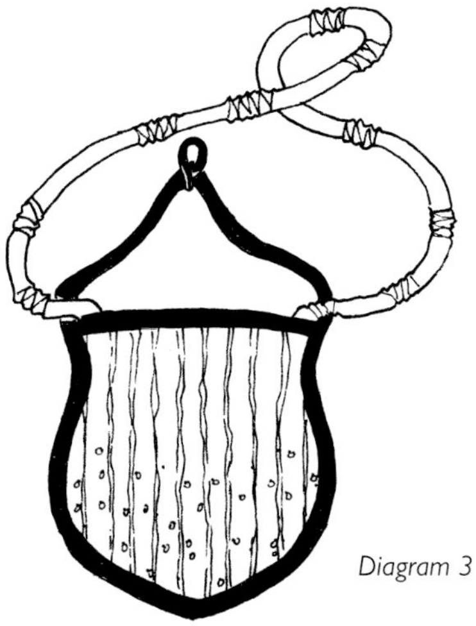
Diagram 3

Diagram 4

Diagrams 1, 2, 3 and 4 show how changing the shape of the flap can alter the appearance of a purse. Two types of handles and different ways of attaching them are also shown.

JOAN MATTHEWS'S PURSE

Joan Matthews has used chamois leather with clay and wooden beads to create a two-sided purse inspired by the craftwork of Native Americans. The surprising combination of leather and a patterned Liberty cotton makes this purse unusual. The two completed sides are stitched together by hand with linen thread, leaving the raw edges of the chamois and the frayed edges of the Liberty cotton free. Long, beaded fringes of cut leather strips and plaited leather with cords of linen thread adorn the purse.

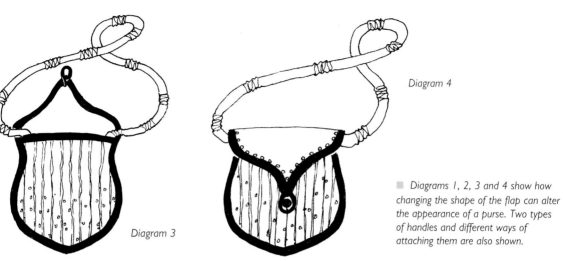

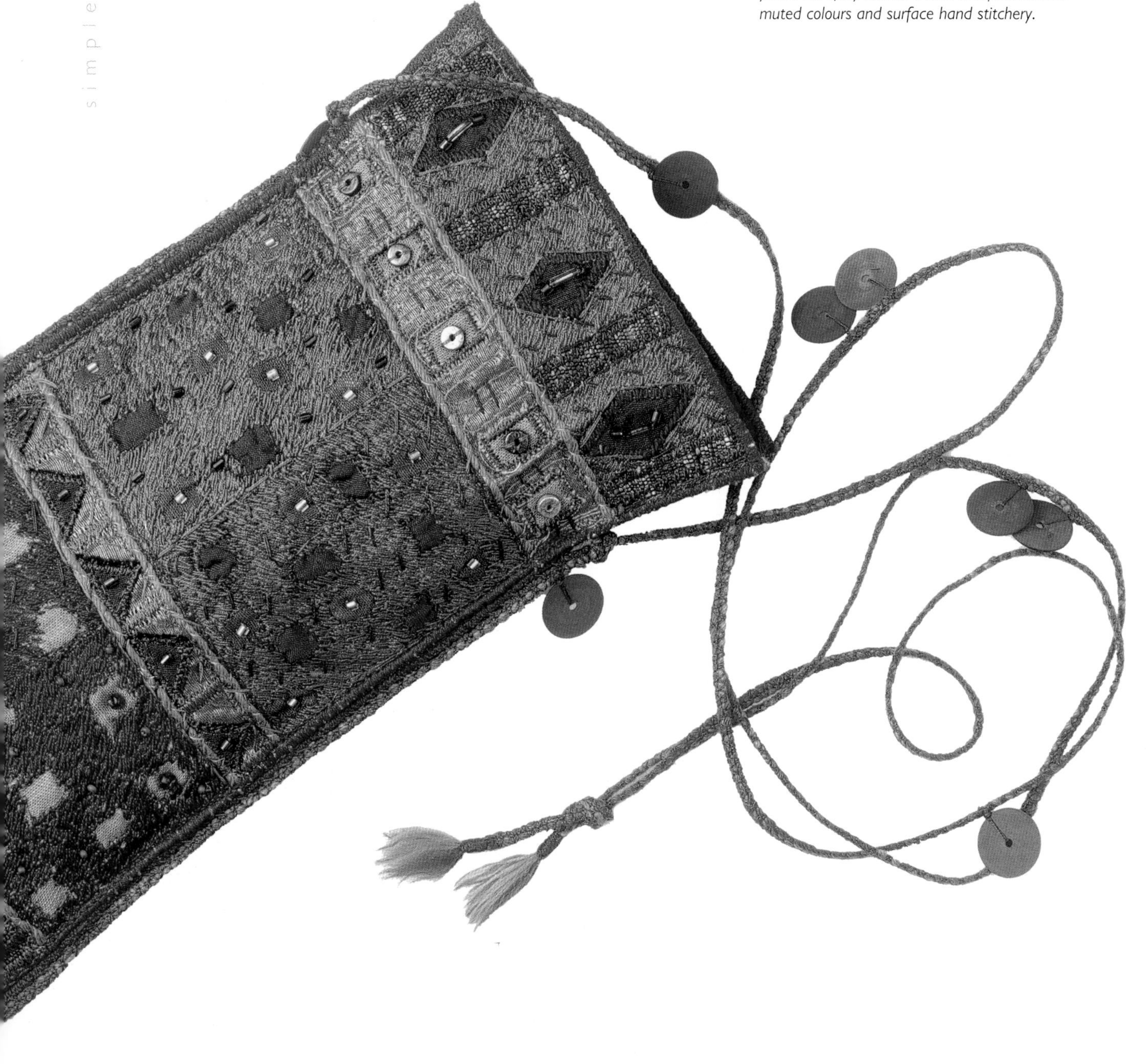

HILARY BOWER'S LONG PURSE
Hilary Bower's long purse, made in 2000, is exquisitely embellished with a wonderful variety of shapes and colours. The two sides are worked differently (see the other side on page 65) with machine embroidery, applied fabrics and couched yarns. Carefully chosen beads complement the muted colours and surface hand stitchery.

KASHMIRI PURSE
The subtle colours of this purse from Kashmir are offset by the dark background. The front and back panels are identical and are entirely covered with chain stitch on a linen ground fabric. Some shapes are outlined with black thread, and some with gold. Each side is lined separately before being stitched together. The side seams stop short of the top edge and the purse is similar in construction to Hilary Bower's purse, on the opposite page.

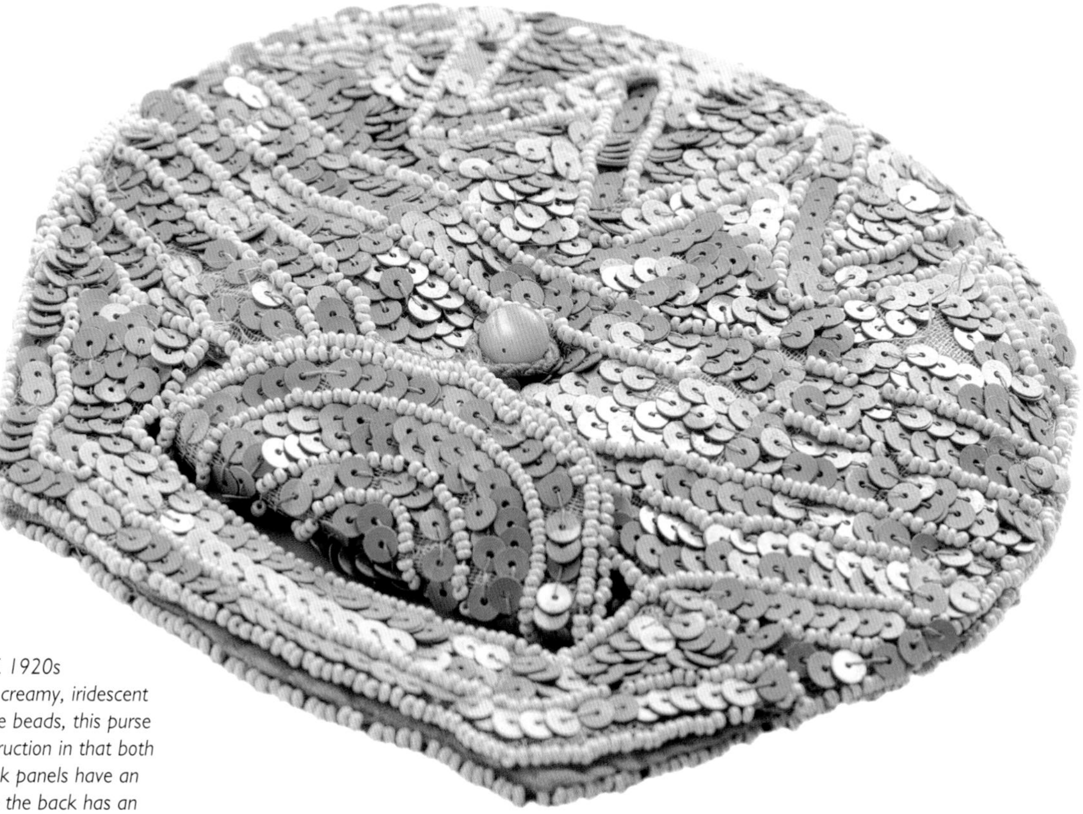

A PURSE FROM THE 1920s
Entirely covered with creamy, iridescent sequins and tiny white beads, this purse has an unusual construction in that both the front and the back panels have an integral handle, while the back has an added flap that folds forwards through the two handles to fasten at the front with a pearl bead.

CHAPTER FIVE FOLDED PURSES

Ancient methods of making purses include simply folding in the corners to envelop precious items . Some are simple embroidered strips folded up and seamed at the sides, like the Rajasthani purse on page 20. The cloth used for folding is often elaborately decorated, and the seams formed by the folding may be generously embellished with clusters of beads or elaborate insertion stitches.

Unlike two-sided purses, in which the front and the back are embroidered, stiffened, lined and bound separately before being stitched together, folded purses can have an integral, continuous lining. In one horizontal piece, the lining is stitched along what will become the top edge of the purse, thus guaranteeing a perfect finish in a critical area. These purses are among the simplest and neatest to make and, as can be seen here, many different effects can be achieved.

The following purses have been inspired by Elizabethan costumes of the 17th century, examples of which can be seen in portrait galleries around the world. The layering of extravagantly decorated fabrics is seductive and, judging by our readiness to embellish, it is perhaps part of the national psyche.

KORAN COVER
This Koran cover has such a rich surface decoration that the red cotton ground fabric is hardly visible. Purses such as this are sometimes described as make-up bags. Now slightly worn in places, it is still a wonderful display of craftsmanship. Stitches include stem stitch, couching, interlacing stitch and shisha work. Red beaded tassels add a third dimension (see page 20 for illustration of whole purse).

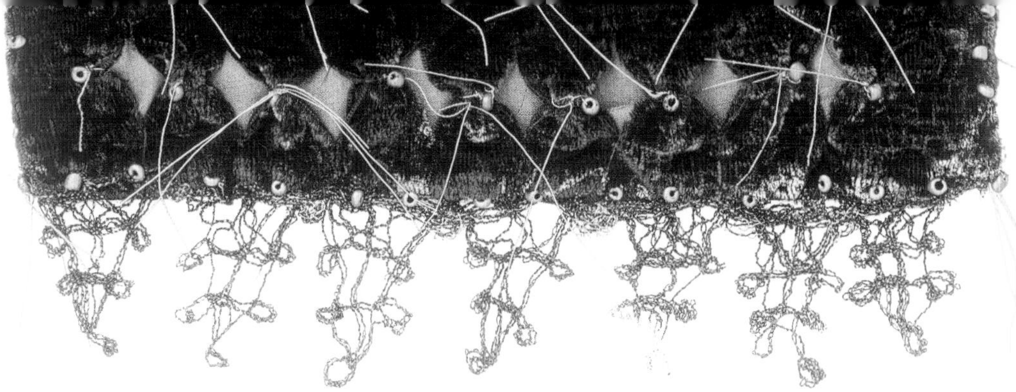

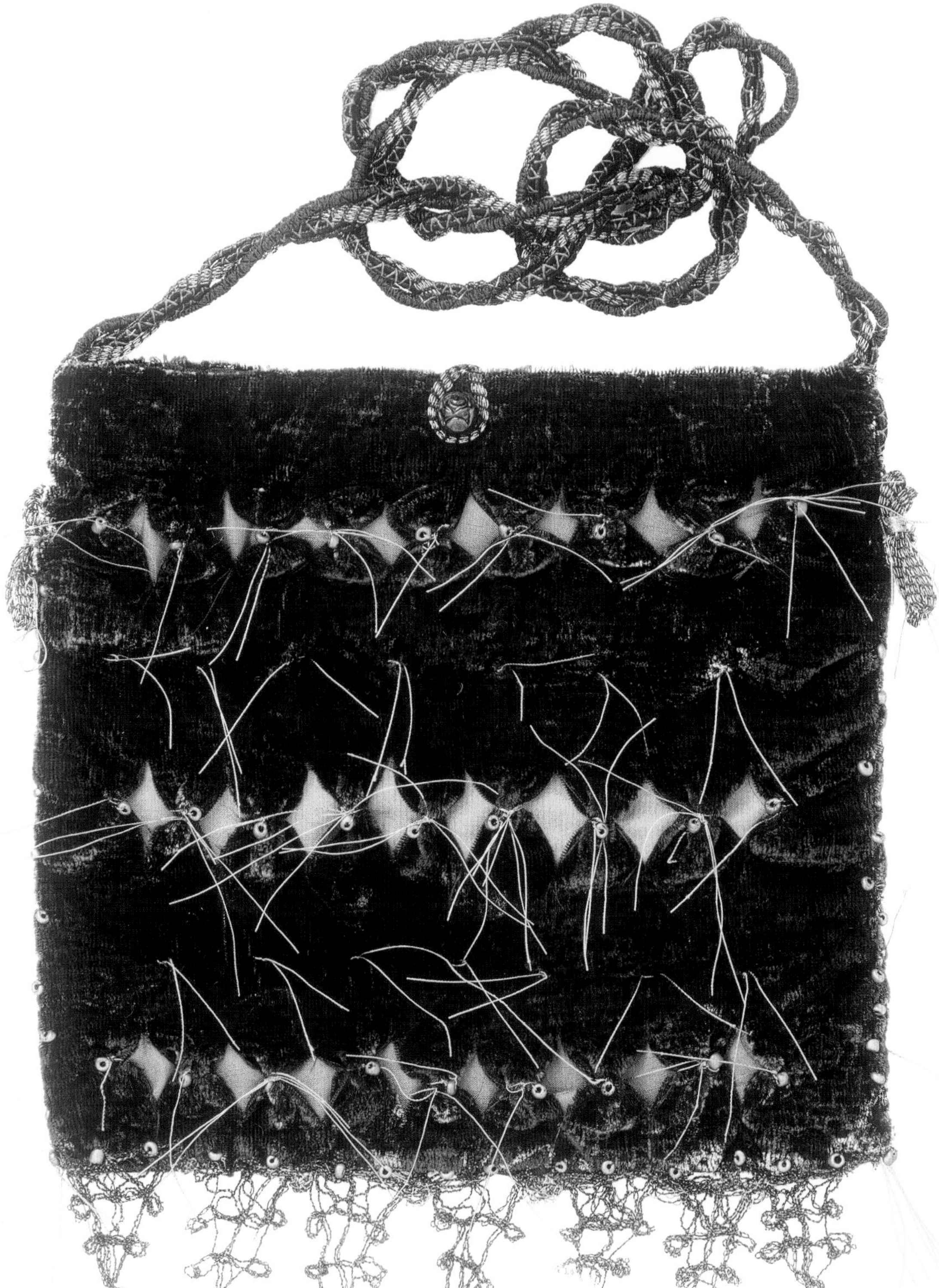

SLASHED VELVET PURSE

In the purse illustrated, velvet was layered with a contrasting silk and decorated generously with gold threads, beads and machine-made lace. The purse has no stiffening, allowing the velvet to drape and fold luxuriously.

Materials

- 50 x 25cm (20 x 10in) velvet
- 50 x 25cm (20 x 10in) silk
- 50 x 25cm (20 x 10in) lining fabric
- a selection of ribbons
- a selection of beads, sequins and metallic threads
- You will also need a rotary cutter, a cutting board, a ruler and a sliver of soap.

Method

1. Take a piece of slashed and tied velvet measuring 20 x 40cm (8 x 16in) (see page 106 for slashing and tying methods) and decorate it lavishly with beads and sequins. Make sure that the size of the beads is appropriate – not too big, in other words – but that there are masses of them to achieve an opulent effect. Stitch a lining of the same size along the top edge and then iron the seam open, taking care not to flatten the velvet (see diagram 1).

2. Lay the joined fabrics flat with the right sides facing up. Bring the short sides up together. Pin and stitch them and trim off any excess, as shown in diagram 2. Gently press the seam open, and turn through. Pass the lining down through the velvet and slipstitch the bottom edges, stitching first the lining and then the velvet.

3. Add handles made of several cords, ribbons or braids twisted together. Stitch one end to each side seam of the purse with finger tassels (see page 115). Using metallic threads, add machined lace (see page 120) to the lower edge (see diagram 3) and a bead to the top edge of the front. Add a short loop of cord to the back of the purse, making it sufficiently long to slip over the bead on the front. The ends of the cord can be stitched in a spiral (see page 123, diagram 56).

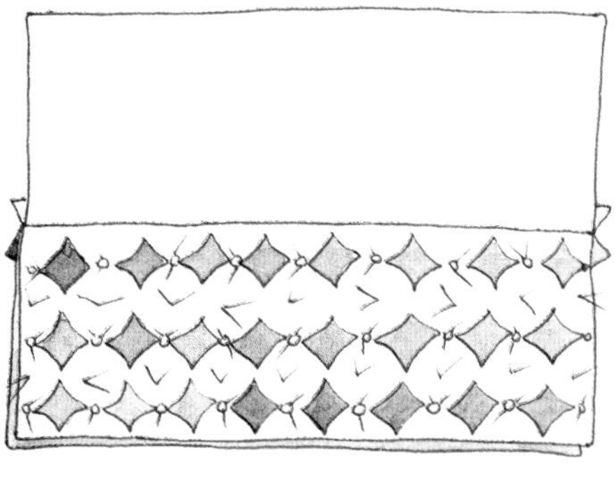

Diagram 1

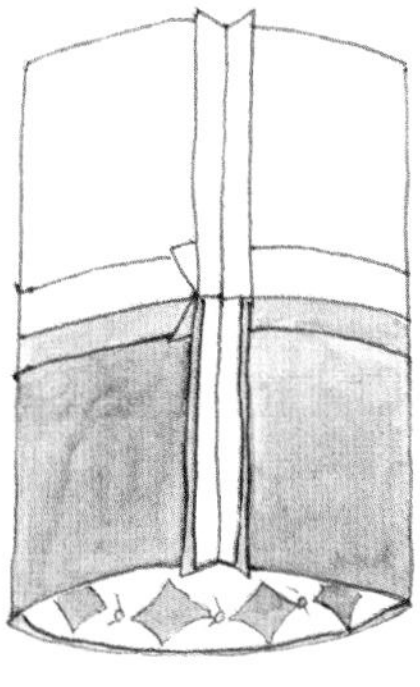

Diagram 2

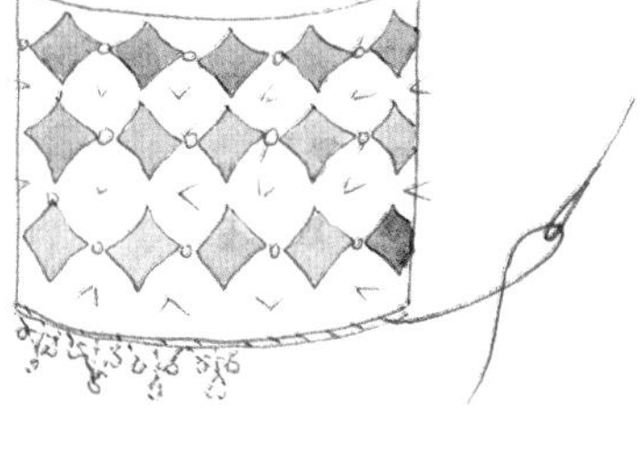

Diagram 3

A PURSE WITH BONDED SILK AND VELVET

Another version of this purse is constructed in the same way, except that the lower edge is stitched to a circular base, giving more room inside and more shape to the outside. Again, the inspiration is the richness of the Elizabethan era, and opulent silk and velvet are therefore used.

This purse was made with a strip of bonded silk and velvet, cut and decorated. It has hand-stitched details and decorated card plaques. Instructions for making card plaques are given on page 111.

Materials

- 23 x 49cm (9 x 15in) velvet
- 46 x 40cm (18 x 15in) contrasting silk
- Small piece pelmet Vilene (Pellon)
- 40 x 13cm (15 x 5in) Bondaweb (Wonder-Under)
- 23 x 10cm (9 x 4in) silk in another colour
- Some small beads
- 10cm (4in) square thick card
- 12 decorated card plaques (see page 111)
- Embroidery threads
- A painted wooden skewer (see page 111)
- 90cm (1yd) string
- Sewing threads to match the fabrics

Method

1. The main body of the purse is made with a strip of bonded and slashed velvet and silk. For full instructions about folding and slashing bonded silk and velvet, see pages 104–105.

2. Take a strip of silk measuring 31cm (12¼in) long and 6cm (2½in) wide. Iron a piece of Bondaweb (Wonder-Under) of the same size to the reverse side. Take a piece of velvet 31cm (12¼in) long and 12cm (5in) wide. Gently bond the silk to the back of the velvet, matching two long edges, and making sure the pile of the velvet is not crushed. Fold the velvet in half lengthways, right side out, and mark diagonal lines at regular intervals with a sliver of soap, avoiding the short ends of the strip to allow for seaming. Cut the marked slanting slashes with sharp scissors. Flatten out the fabrics and gently fold back the cut velvet to reveal the silk. Secure each folded-back triangular flap with a stitch or bead. Place a contrasting coloured strip of silk the same length and 6cm (2½in) wide under the slashes and secure with running stitches on both sides of the cuts.

3. Further embellish the surface liberally with rows of decorated card plaques, beads and pieces cut from the painted wooden skewer.

4. Now, cut a circle of card, 9cm (3½in) in diameter, for the base of the purse. To cover the base with silk, cut two circles of silk fabric to the same size but with a 1cm (⅜in) seam allowance all around. Place the card in the centre of one circle and glue the seam allowance down as shown in diagram 1, page 56. Stitch the other circle, placed on the other side of the card, to the glued fabric, turning in the seam allowance (see diagram 2, page 56).

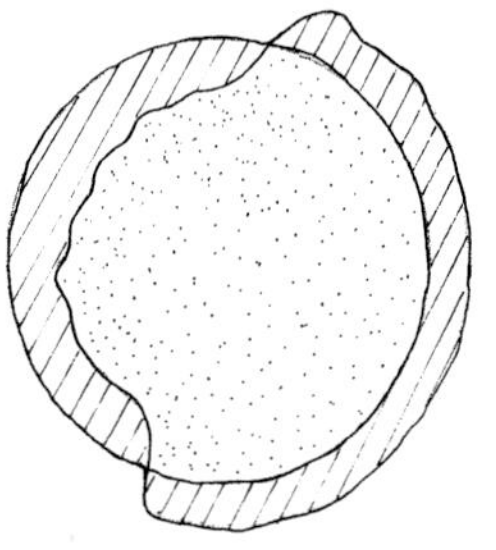

Diagram 1

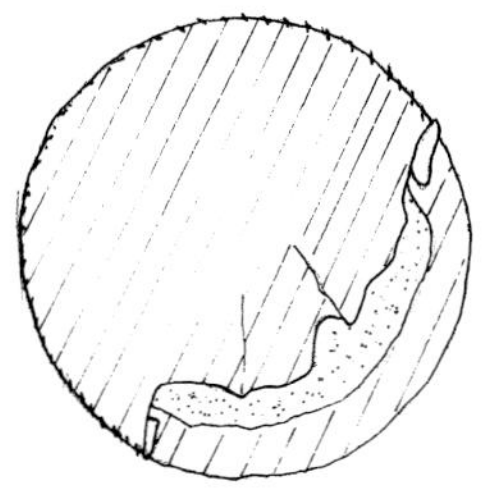

Diagram 2

5. To construct the purse, seam a piece of silk lining fabric 19cm ($7\frac{1}{2}$in) wide and the same length as the velvet along the top edge of the velvet strip, as shown in diagram 3. Fold the joined piece in half, right sides together, and stitch the ends with a 1cm ($\frac{3}{8}$in) seam allowance, to form a tube (see diagram 4). Turn right sides out and slip the silk lining down into the purse, leaving a border to show at the top edge. Turn the lower edge of the lining up and slipstitch to the lower edge of the velvet (see diagram 5).

6. Slipstitch the base to the lower edge. Attach machined-cord handles (see page 108) to the sides, and cover the ends with card plaques.

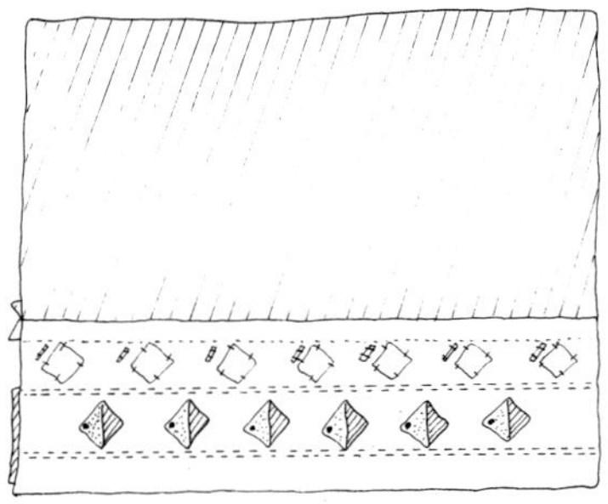

Diagram 3

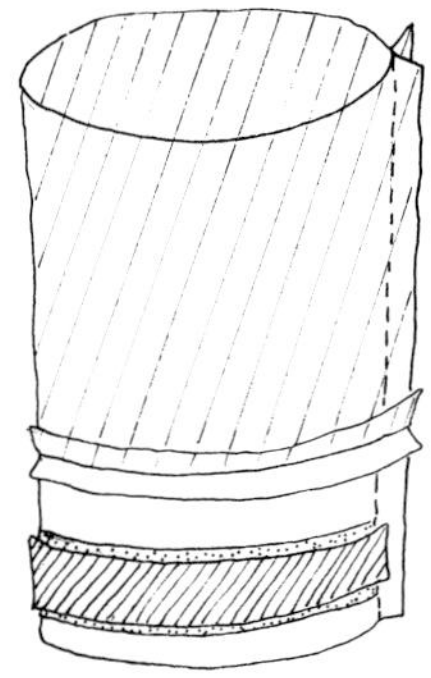

Diagram 4

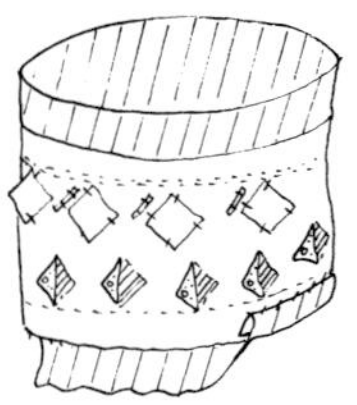

Diagram 5

7. To make a tab with a contrasting edge, cut a piece of pelmet Vilene (Pellon) to the required size. Cover and stitch the Vilene shape, incorporating bound edges (see page 104) in a contrasting colour all around the edge. Attach the finished tab by stitching to the back of the purse.

BLACK VELVET PRINTED PURSE

The purse below is made using a similar method to the purse on page 52. First the velvet was printed with gold metallic fabric paints using cork printing blocks. Machine embroidery, beads and sequins were used to further embellish the printed surface. The finished strip was stitched to a lining of yellow silk that was cut 1cm (3⁄8in) deeper than the velvet to allow a top yellow margin. A handle of twisted cords was stitched at each side in a spiral, making a feature of the attachment.

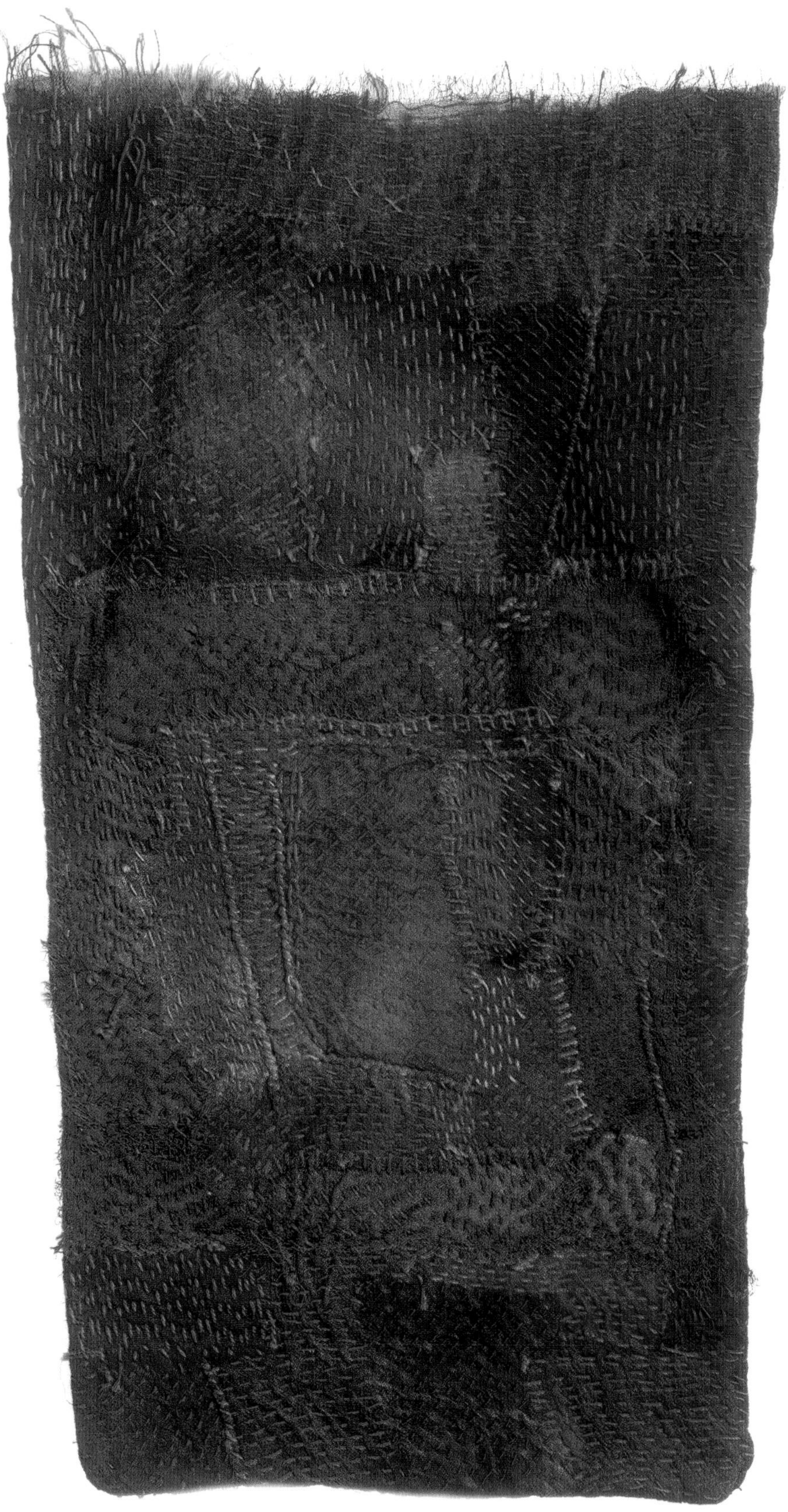

JENNY BULLEN'S PURSE
This purse, 26.5cm (10½in) long by 13.5cm (5¼in) wide, was made by Jenny Bullen and illustrates the folded purse in its simplest form. Just as in many of the purses from the Indian subcontinent, the major part of the work has been invested in the embroidery, keeping the construction to a minimum to stunning effect. Entirely hand-stitched through layers of hand-dyed silk organza arranged on dyed butter-muslin, it evokes images of ancient, fragmentary textiles. It has been worked with the simplest of stitches: running, blanket, over-sewing and cross. The rich colours of the fabrics and threads shimmer across the surface. Exquisite all-over decoration such as this needs only the simplest of construction. The layered and stitched square has been folded and seamed at the back and at the slightly narrower base. The wider top has been left as a delicately frayed edge.

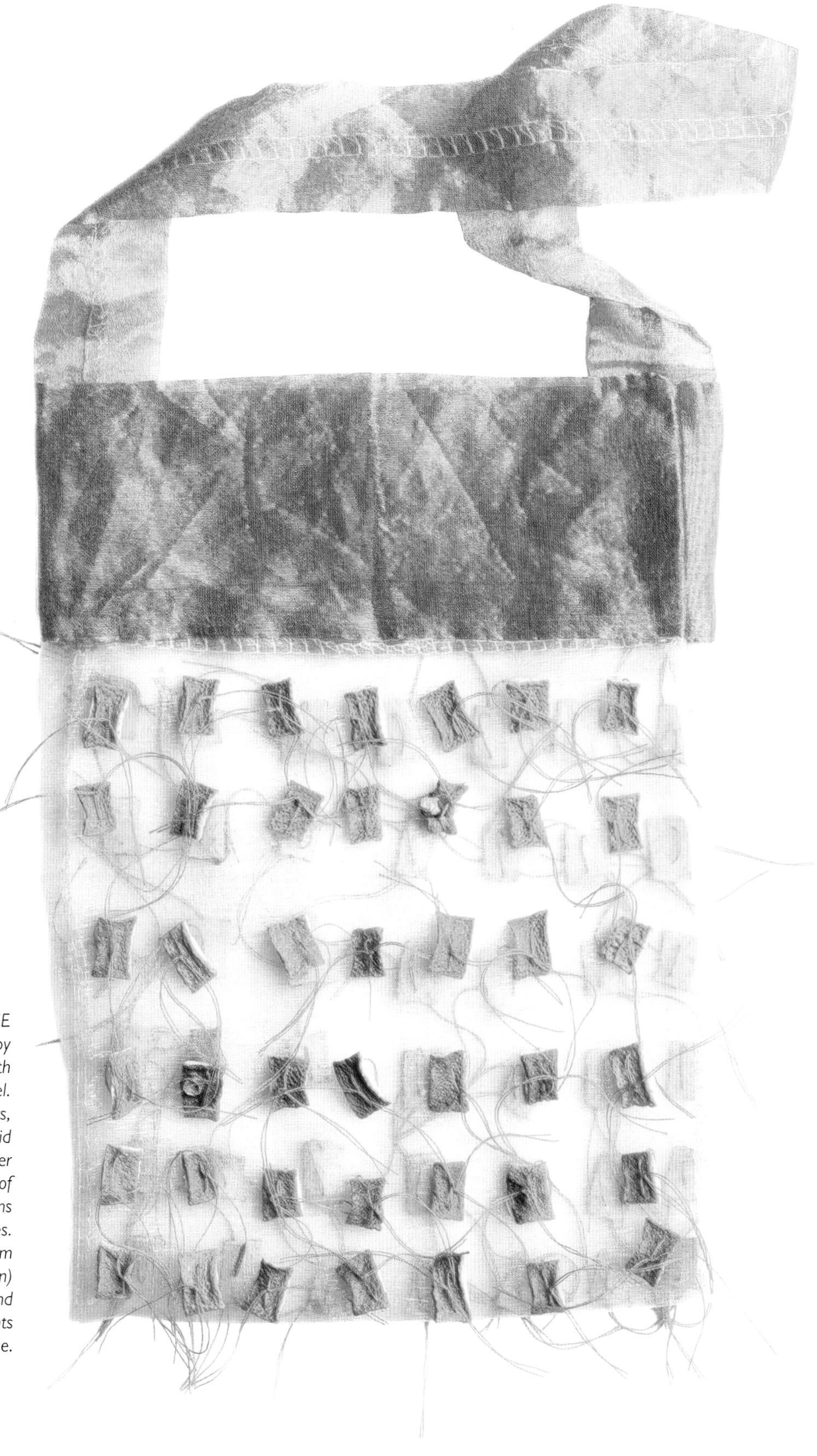

JENNIFER COLLIER'S PURSE
This exquisite purse, made by Jennifer Collier, is created with organza and dried lemon peel. The peel is cut into oblongs, dried and attached with a grid of cotton thread to polyester organza. A wide band of metallic silk organza forms the top and handles. The purse measures 22cm (8½in) long and 15cm (6in) wide. The use of colour and balance of design elements create a very pleasing purse.

Working in a series

If a design source is so inspirational that you work with it and use it perhaps for several months or even years, then you may wish to make a series of purses, developing work on the same theme. In this way, you can build on your knowledge of a subject, allowing continuity of thought and furthering the development of ideas. This process allows you to probe deeper into the subject and to extract the less obvious and perhaps the more subtle elements of the source. It also allows the development of a personal style.

It is useful, when working in this way, to surround yourself with a display of the theme by pinning up postcards and cuttings, drawings and paintings, samples and ideas on a pin board. Such a display is not only inspiring in itself, but by looking at it, it is possible to see the work in a new light, to see connections and possibilities.

The four purses featured on pages 62–63 were made in response to work using the sea as a design source. A limited pallet of five or six colours was chosen. These were gleaned from studies of the colours of waves on winter days – charcoal, gun-metal grey, turquoise, white and black. They were combined with tiny details of sail-stitching and shapes gleaned from observations of boats made over a long period of time.

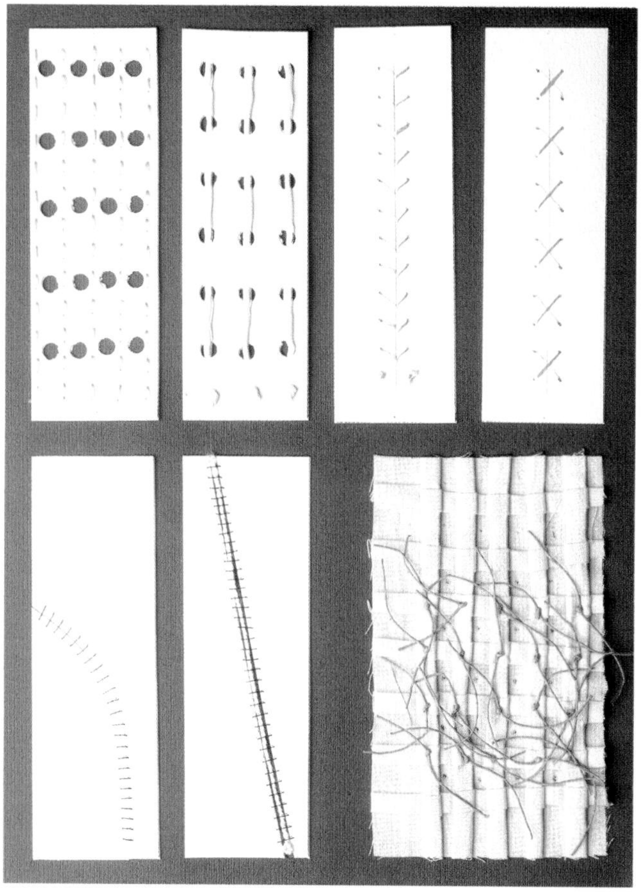

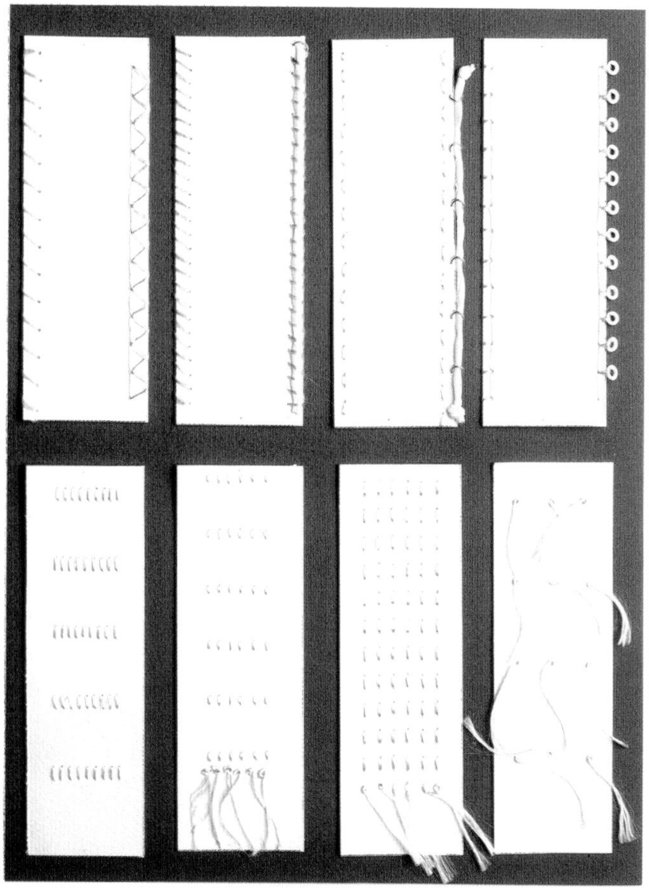

Sketchbooks of drawings and folders of photographs were gathered together and samples of stitching and beading were worked on the edges of pieces of watercolour paper. Silk threads, beads, paper, string and rouleaux were used, all in monochrome (see opposite).

Next, swatches of coloured fabrics and threads and some beads were gathered, many being discarded as unsuitable in the process. Finally, a few cotton and linen materials were chosen, these being the closest to 'sailcloth', along with circular, plate-like beads suggestive of portholes and of the rings found on rigging. The identical overall shape of the purses was kept deliberately simple in order to concentrate attention on the decoration.

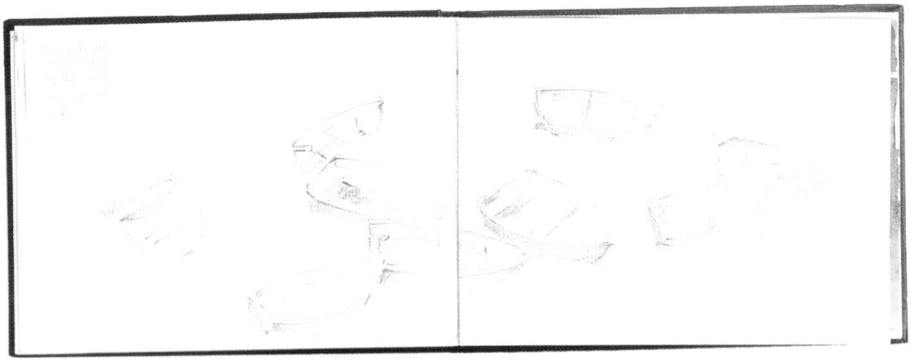

Drawings of boats turning on their moorings on the incoming tide, and images of rigging of all kinds, enabled me to get to know my subject more closely.

Opposite page ▪ Boat rigging and stitching on sails, wind indicators and methods of lashing masts are all sampled with silk threads and string on watercolour paper.

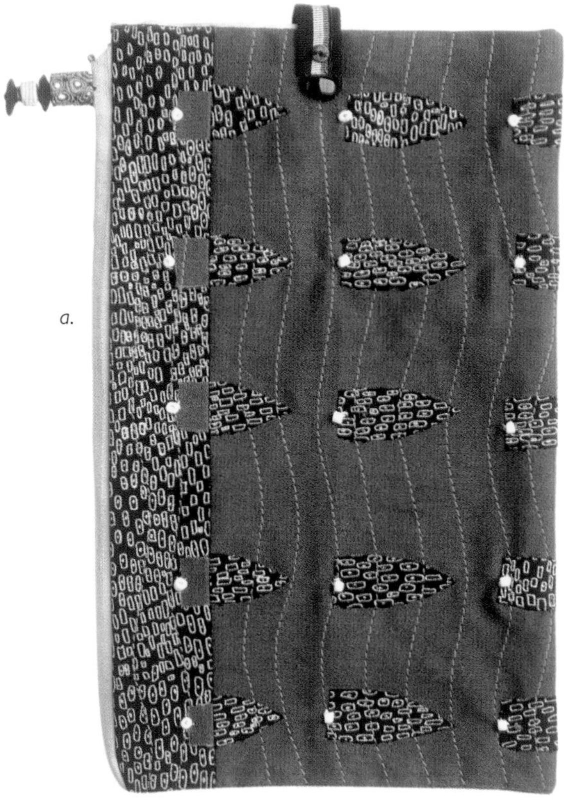
a.

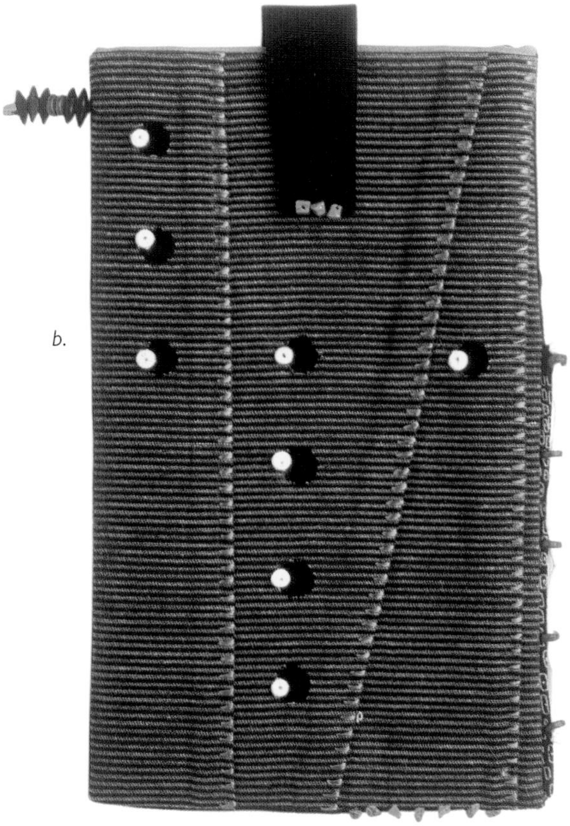
b.

WORKING IN A SERIES: THE PURSES

a. Battleship-grey cotton has applied boat shapes arranged in lines like those in a marina. The boats are in a cotton fabric reminiscent of rocky shorelines. A thin turquoise strip has been let into the left-hand seam and a string of rock-like beads attached at the top. A tab made of old kimono fabric finishes the purse.

b. Thinly striped fabric was folded, pressed and stitched with small horizontal stitches reminiscent of sections of a sail. Several 'portholes' were cut and the fabric bonded to an underlying black cotton. Beads were added and a thin strip of patterned fabric let into the side seam. V-shaped cuts were made in the thin strip, and a wire was passed down, threading through a horizontal bead at each cut (see page 112, diagram 29). A white rouleaux was passed down through the beads like the rigging on a yacht. A tab and further beads were added to finish the purse.

c.

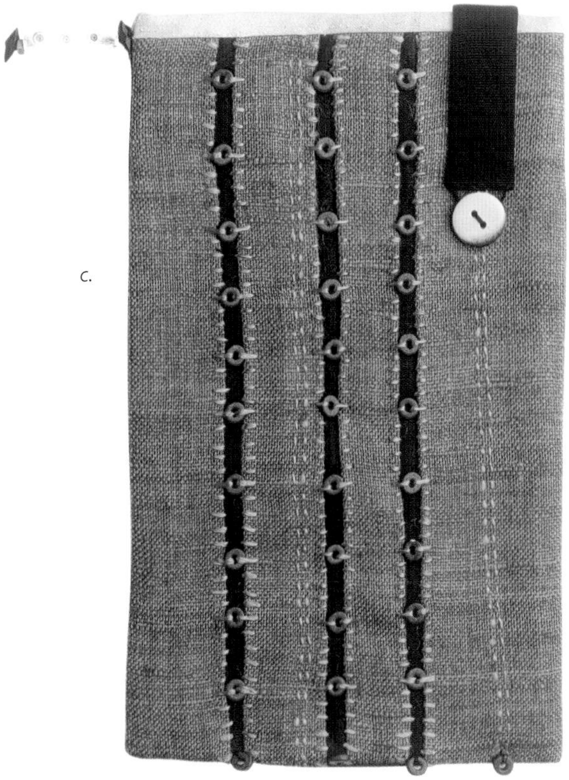

d.

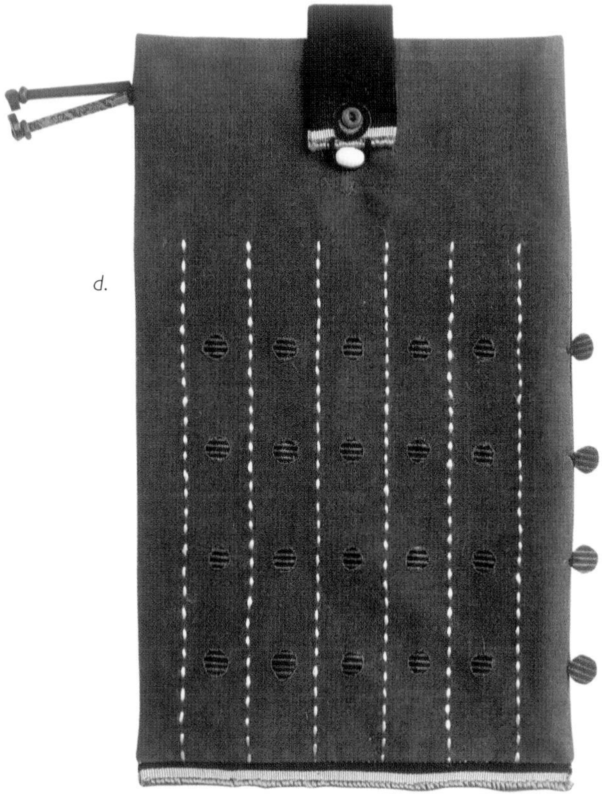

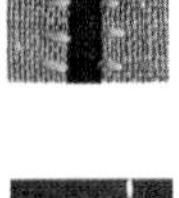

c. The edges of strips of linen were turned in and secured with small horizontal stitches and beads reminiscent of the edges of sails. The gaps between the strips were backed with black cotton. The purse was further enhanced with beads and simple running stitch.

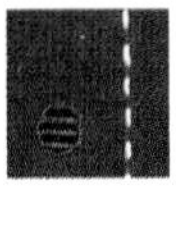

d. Porthole-like circles were cut in a grid arrangement and bonded to stripy material. Simple running stitch was worked in vertical lines and bonded, and cut discs of fabric were arranged down the edge of the purse. A strip of old kimono fabric was used along the bottom edge and to make a tab with a nautical flavour. Long beads were attached at the top corner.

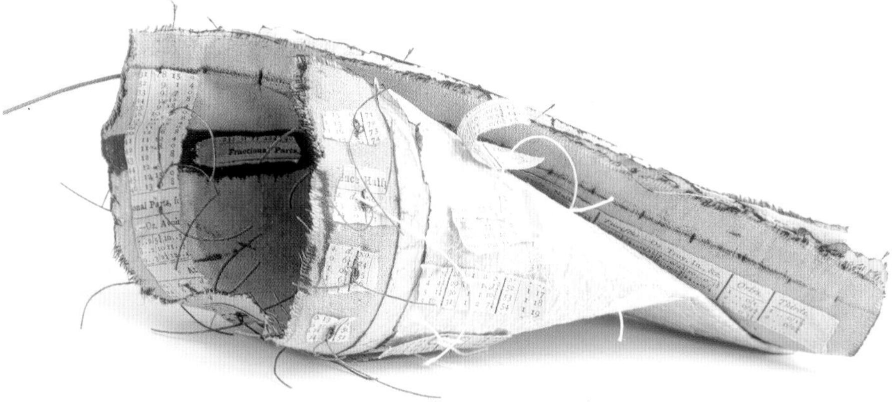

JAN MILLER'S SWEET PURSES

Jan Miller's creations are based on the notion of sweet purses and memories of childhood trips to the corner shop to buy penny sweets, with names such as Black Jack and Fruit Salad. The sweets were enclosed in kite-shaped paper bags, the ends folded up by the shopkeeper to form a container. Jan has manipulated old linen and paper together to form a layered funnel, the pointed base folded up to seal the end. Torn fragments of text from a Ready Reckoner, like the one used by the shopkeeper, along with wire, ink and linen thread, embellish the surfaces. These purses not only represent childhood memories, but also resonate with echoes of the sweet purses that were made as special gift wrappings in the 17th century and the simple folding of flat, decorated surfaces so often used to great effect in non-western cultures.

HILARY BOWER'S LONG PURSE
Hilary Bower's most recent work is in the form of pouch structures that hang from the wall and are direct 'descendants' of her earlier purses (see page 34), manifesting the development of an idea through years of research and refinement. The purse shown here, made in 2000, is exquisitely machine-stitched and embroidered in muted colours. Each side is worked differently, with a machine-embroidered ground, sometimes leaving small areas unworked. Hand stitching, beads and couched yarns add to the gorgeous surface decoration. A machined-cord handle extends around the purse and is knotted at each side, just below the opening. See the whole purse on page 48.

CHAPTER SIX CLUTCH PURSES

Clutch purses have always been popular, but were especially so in the 1920s and 1930s, when they were also called 'pochettes'. Women's magazines of the time have numerous patterns and sets of instructions for making pochettes, some novelty ones, others with Egyptian-inspired decorations or Art Deco designs. Unusual clutch purses were all the rage, some of these being in the shape of cars or ocean-going liners. They were popular, and convenient too, as they tucked under the arm, leaving the hands free for dealing with cigarettes and cocktails.

Despite their limited size, many surviving examples of pochettes from the 1920s and 1930s contain mirrors and coin purses. Some have separate compartments for lipstick and comb as well, a far cry from the days when all a girl needed was a tiny coin purse or a two-inch embroidered purse to hold her dance card. Since the 1930s, clutch purses have continued to be popular, especially for evening wear, possibly because they have no straps or handles to distort the shape of the outfit they accompany.

Whereas folded purses are made from strips folded vertically and then seamed, clutch purses are folded horizontally and both sides stitched. Ingenious methods have been devised to incorporate pockets within the purses, by folding the elongated lining one or more times before the sides are stitched (see page 71).

1920s AUSTRIAN PURSE
This professionally made pochette or clutch purse, complete with mirror, coin purse and press-stud fastener, is identical at the front and back. The design resembles a rug and is worked in minute tent stitch, with 32 stitches to the inch. It was probably made in Austria, where a thriving industry also made beaded clutch purses in Art Deco designs as well as those taken from rugs. It is stiffened with card and the work is lightly padded.

CORAL AND BLUE CHINESE CLUTCH PURSE
This purse has been constructed from a reused textile. Possibly made in a workshop in the Far East, it has been stiffened with card and lined with silk. Inside are many useful compartments, including one for a mirror and a small coin purse. Although the outside is now faded, the beautiful coral-coloured Chinese tassels add a touch of glamour.

SEA-INSPIRED CHINESE SILK PURSES

The clutch purses featured here were made using drawings of shells and seaweed. The fabric, a hand-dyed Chinese silk satin, is soft and has a beautiful sheen. It is consequently ideal for quilting. Skinned wadding, manufactured especially for garments, was used. The shapes on the flaps are bonded appliqué (see page 70). When backed with Bondaweb (Wonder-Under), intricate shapes can be cut out, even from fabric as soft as this. The seaweed motif used was the negative shape left after the seaweed was cut out. The positive shape was used in another purse, so there is no waste whatsoever. Despite the slight stiffening that occurs when fabric is bonded, the shapes are hand-quilted and beaded.

Materials

- 50 x 30cm (20 x 12in) silk fabric
- 50 x 30cm (20 x 12in) skinned wadding
- 50 x 30cm (20 x 12in) lining fabric
- Small piece Bondaweb (Wonder-Under)
- Selection of silk scraps for appliqué
- Selection of beads
- Approximately 1m (1yd) braid or ribbon for fastening and tassels

Method

1. To make a similar purse, first make a paper pattern. The clutch purses seen here were each made with a rectangle of fabric measuring 40cm x 20cm (16 x 8in) including 1cm (⅜in) seam allowances. To make the purse with the curved flap, one of the short ends should be cut as a semi-circle.

2. Using your paper pattern, cut one piece from the top fabric, marking the folds. Bond appliqué shapes to the flap area. Cut a piece of skinned wadding to the same size and tack (baste) it to the top fabric. Quilt and bead the appliquéd design.

3. Now cut a lining to the same shape and size as the top, marking folds. Place it on top of the right side of the appliquéd piece and stitch together at the short ends, positioning a loop in the centre of the flap seam. Trim wadding away at the seams (see diagram 1).

4. Pull the lining away from the outer fabric and line up the stitched seams. Stitch the two side seams of the outer fabric and trim the wadding to minimize bulk, as shown in diagram 2. Turn through the open lining seams. Turn in seam allowances and slipstitch the side seams. Push the lining down into the purse, making sure the seams with the lining meet.

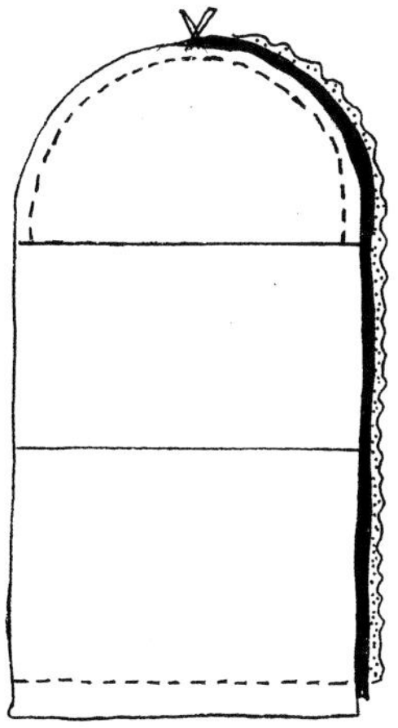

Diagram 1

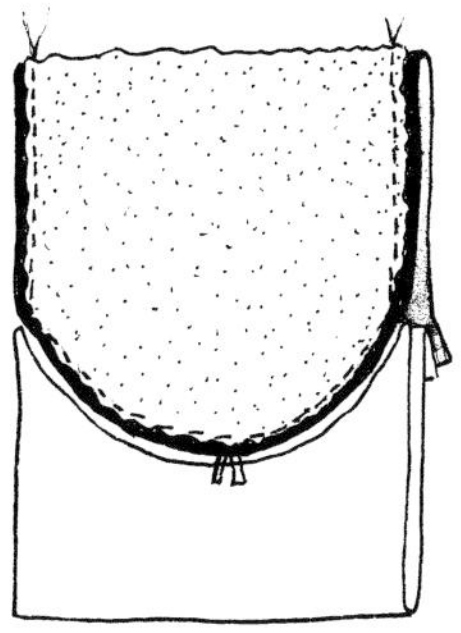

Diagram 2

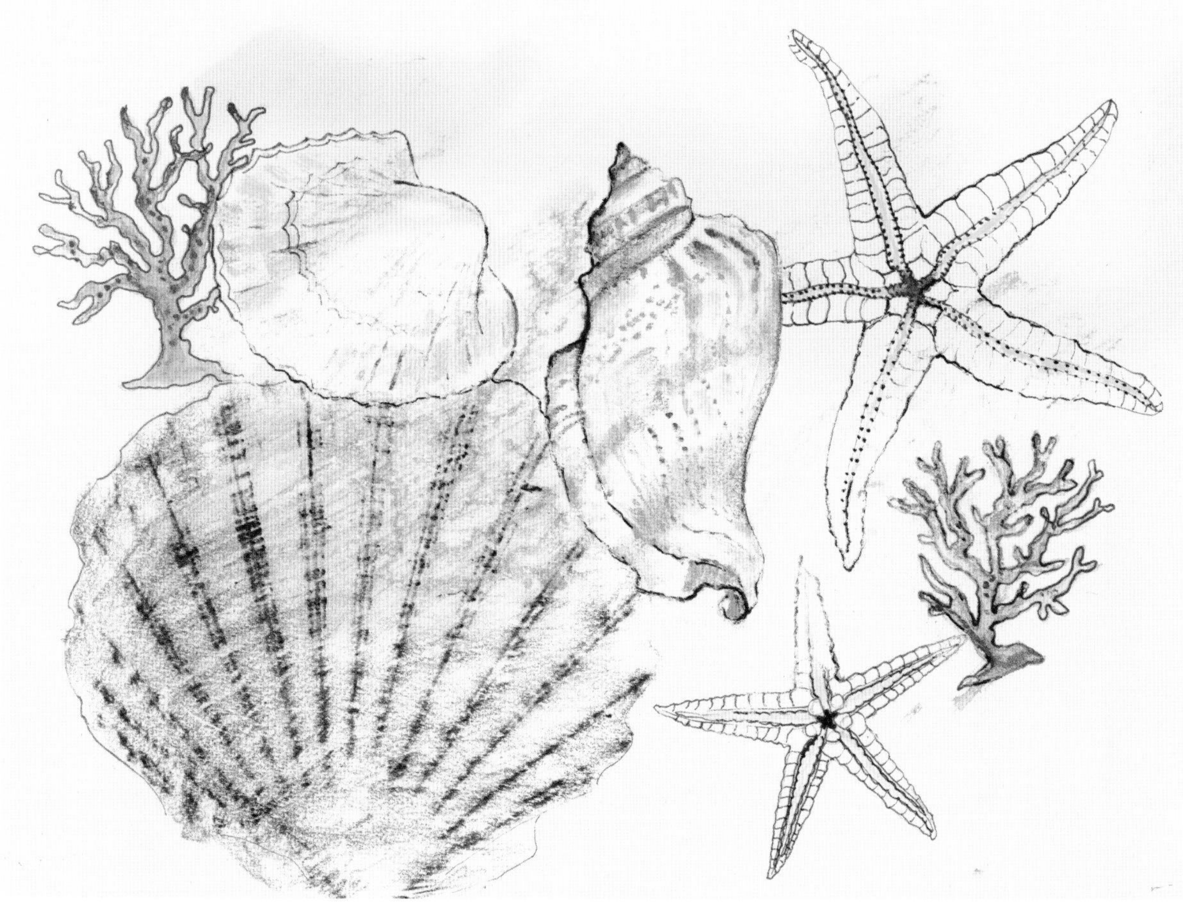

Sea-inspired designs in a sketchbook.

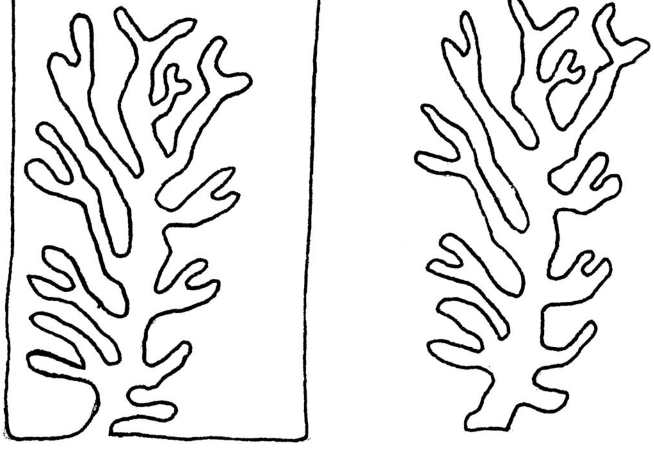

The negative shape on the left was used in the purse shown on page 68, while the positive shape was used elsewhere.

Making pockets

To make pockets inside a clutch purse, use the same procedure but make the lining extra long. Mark the folds on the top fabric. With right sides together, sew the top and lining fabrics at the top and bottom (short) edges, as shown in diagram 1, starting and ending these seams at the 1cm (⅜in) seam allowance. Trim any seam allowance to minimize bulk.

Turn right sides out, press seams and turn inside out again. Take the bottom seam up between the lining and top fabric to the mark for the flap. Pass the extra lining fabric up to form the pocket(s), as shown in diagram 2. Pin through all layers and stitch the side seams, starting and ending at the previously stitched seams. Leave a small gap in the flap (see diagram 3). Trim the corners and turn the fabrics right side out through the gap. Slipstitch the opening.

Diagram 1

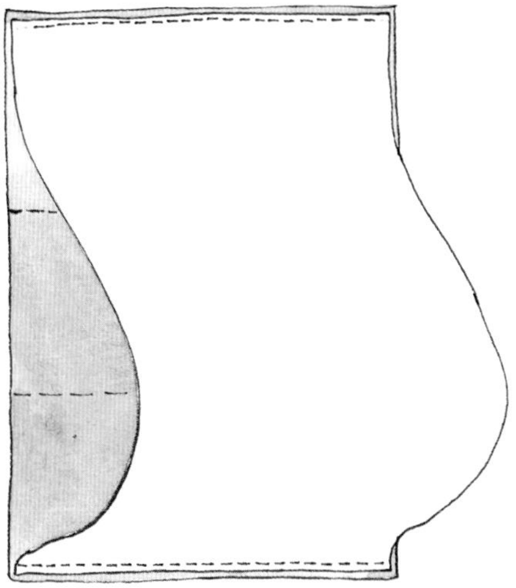

Diagram 2

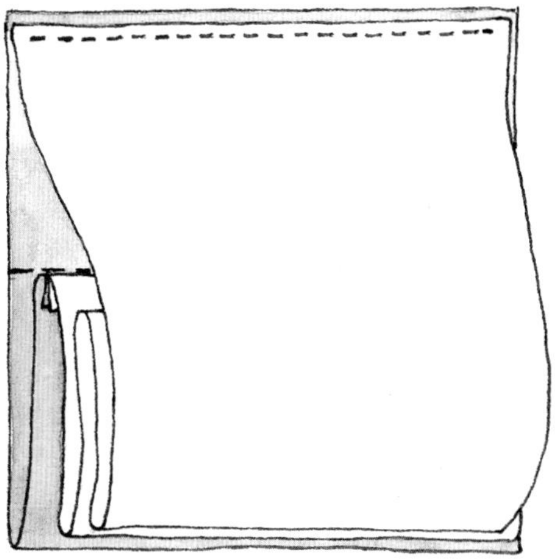

Diagram 3

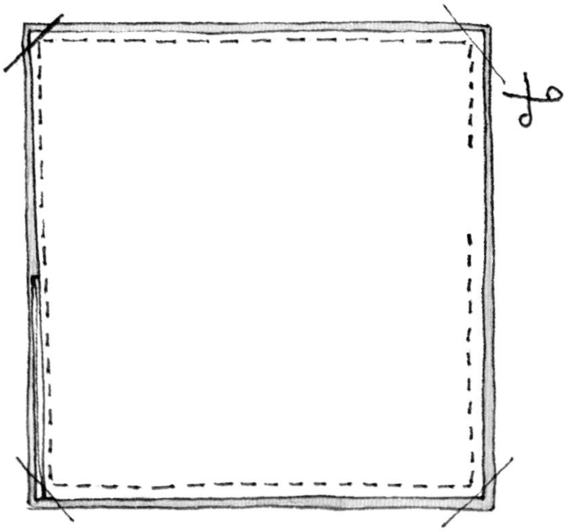

PURSE FROM KASHMIR
This Kashmiri purse is made from a long strip, folded in three, the top section forming the flap. It is embroidered with silk threads on a cotton ground in satin and straight stitch, with a symmetrical pattern of flowers, leaves and paisley shapes arranged to fit the shape of the purse. It has been much used and is slightly worn.

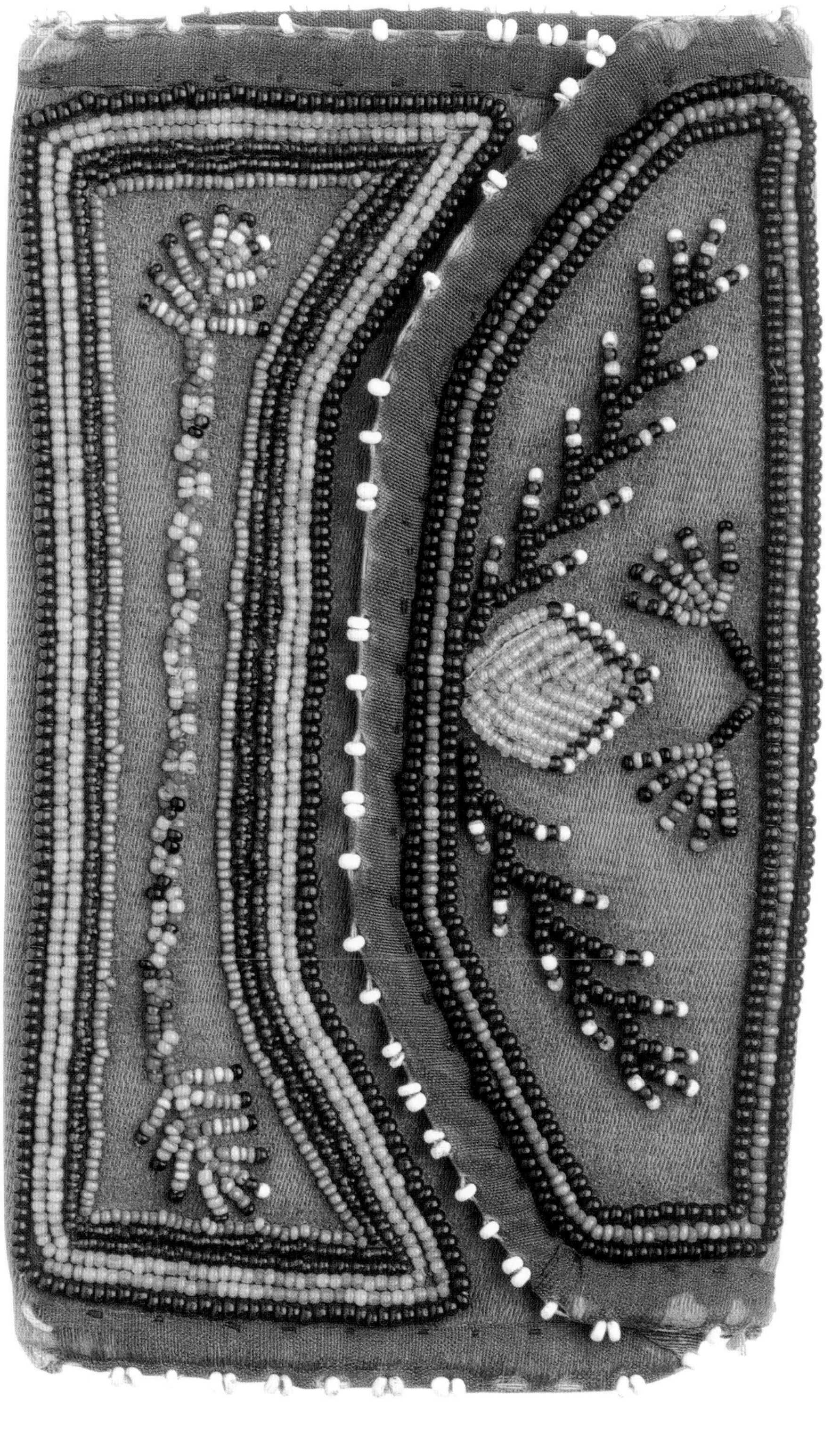

NATIVE AMERICAN PURSE
This delightful purse, 7cm (2¾in) deep and 11.5cm (4½in), wide comes from the USA and is made from buckskin. It is constructed from a strip folded into three, with pockets inside. The sides are not stitched together. It was made by Native Americans in the last half of the 19th century, when embroideries incorporating pink and blue seed beads proliferated. Several beads were strung together on a needle and couched down with the same thread to produce long straight lines.

CHAPTER SEVEN PURSES WITH GUSSETS

Most handbags and many purses have gussets, to allow more room inside and an enlarged space for access through the opening. Gussets can be simple strips stitched between the front and back panels and ending at the top edge, or they can be strips that are not only gussets but form the handle as well, in one continuous strip.

Gussets can be shaped, as in the purse shown on page 78. Here, the gusset enhances the overall shape of the purse by adding a varying depth to the sides, narrowing at the point where the tassel is attached and widening at the middle of the purse. Gussets can also be added in pairs, as in the purse opposite. Here, the gussets are V-shaped and slightly curved at the top edges so that when the purse is closed, they fold inwards. In some purses, gussets are stitched into each side of a continuous front and back piece.

Gussets need to be stiffened in some way. Those in larger bags are stiffened with card or buckram. For smaller pieces, lighter stiffenings can be used and the type will depend on the fabrics employed. For instance, in the purse shown on page 78, the silk used for the gusset needed only to be bonded to a second layer of silk to achieve sufficient body to avoid sagging. For heavier fabrics there are several weights of iron-on Vilene (Pellon) and it is always best to sample first using oddments of the purse fabric.

It is a good idea to try out shapes for purses in paper first (see page 77) and it is even more important to carry out this process as purses become more complicated in their construction. In this way all the problems of shapes, fastenings and handle attachments can be worked out using paper and string before you embark on the stitching of fabrics. Many pitfalls can be avoided and, most importantly, you will learn whether the pieces will fit together and produce the required shape.

1920s GUSSETED PURSE
This 1920s purse has a soft, pleasing shape. The flowers and leaves are embroidered on black grosgrain using chain stitch in muted colours. They are surrounded by masses of grey-white beads arranged within a scrolled border. The flap is fastened with a press-stud. The purse appears to have been well used and the interior is in a poor state of repair as a result, whereas the exterior, with its hard-wearing fabric and beads, seems as fresh as the day it was made.

A GUSSETED CANVASWORK PURSE
Measuring 12½cm (5in) long, this purse has two canvaswork panels worked in different patterns in tent stitch in wool. Each panel is stiffened and slightly padded, with different patterns on each side. It has an unusual construction. Each side has two holes for the metal thread drawstring, which then passes through metal rings in the blue silk gusset, which is in a fragile state. (Embroiderers' Guild)

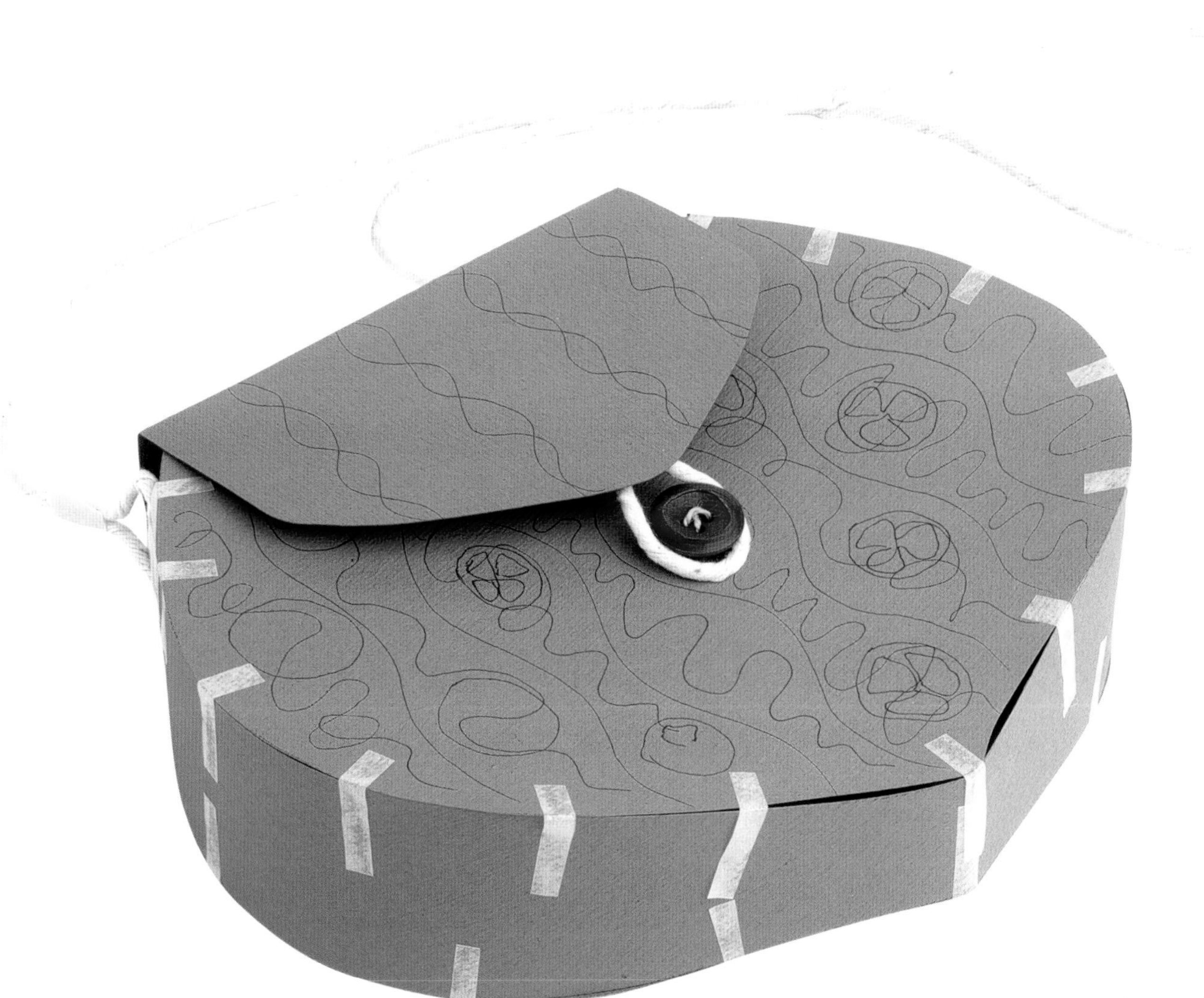

Paper mock-up of purse with gusset

Mock-up for a purse with a gusset

To make a mock-up for a gusseted purse, use paper with body, such as brown wrapping paper or cartridge paper. Masking tape cut into strips is ideal for sticking the pieces together as it can be unstuck and repositioned when necessary. Household string can be used to represent any handles, cords or fastenings. The positioning of the handles, how they are to be attached and whether the point of attachment should be concealed or made into a feature, can all be considered and solved. The type of fastening to be used can also be worked out at this stage, along with alternative sizes of bead or button used for the fastening and the size of any tassels (see page 114–117).

It is even a good idea to draw out the positioning of the embroidery on the purse, to ensure that it is not obscured by the flap. In the paper purse illustrated, the decision was taken to echo the embroidery on the front of the purse in a simplified form on the flap. It was also decided to stitch the front and back panels together at the point where the tassel is attached, as it further enhanced the shape of the purse (see page 78). Several different sizes of tassel were tried out before deciding on the largest one. The handle is looped over a long bead at each side of the purse, thus using the space afforded by the top of the gusset.

This paper mock-up is the model for the purse in the project that immediately follows.

GUSSETED PURSE

The inspiration for this purse came from images of microscopic marine life, while the colours were taken from the bead used as a fastening. Hand-dyed Habotai silk was layered with three other silk fabrics and then machine-stitched in wavy lines and circles, reminiscent of plankton. The fabrics were then cut through to reveal glimpses of the layers underneath. Further machine stitching in metallic threads and couched imitation jap gold enhance the surface. The purse measures 16cm (6½in) by 14cm (5½in). It has a front section, a back section which extends over the front as a flap, and a shaped gusset. The sections are made and lined separately then joined together and the edges bound with crossways binding.

Materials

- 50 x 50cm (20 x 20in) silk fabric
- 3 x 20cm (8in) squares silk fabrics in contrasting colours
- 50cm (20in) square pelmet Vilene (Pellon)
- 50 x 50cm (20 x 10in) lining fabric
- 50 x 20cm (20 x 10in) Bondaweb (Wonder-Under)
- 140cm (55in) crossways binding, 2.5cm (1in) wide
- 50 small beads and 1 large bead
- Metallic machine embroidery threads
- 2m (2⅛yd) Jap gold thread
- Ribbon
- 1m (1yd) thick soft cord
- 2 pieces silk, each 40 x 6.5cm (16 x 2½ in), in a contrasting colour
- Bondaweb to match
- 23 x 36cm (9 x 14in) finely pleated silk

Method

1. First cut out the front and back panels in pelmet Vilene (Pellon) (see diagrams 1 and 2). Bond a piece of silk to the back section and machine-embroider in curvy lines, using metallic threads. Mark the centre front of the flap. Bond lining to both the front and back sections. Cut two pieces of silk for the gusset and bond them together. Bind the short ends with small strips of contrasting fabric and mark the centre of the gusset, as shown in diagram 3.

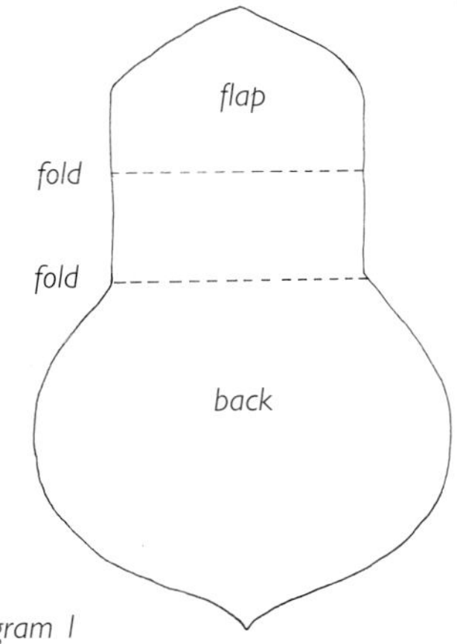

Diagram 1

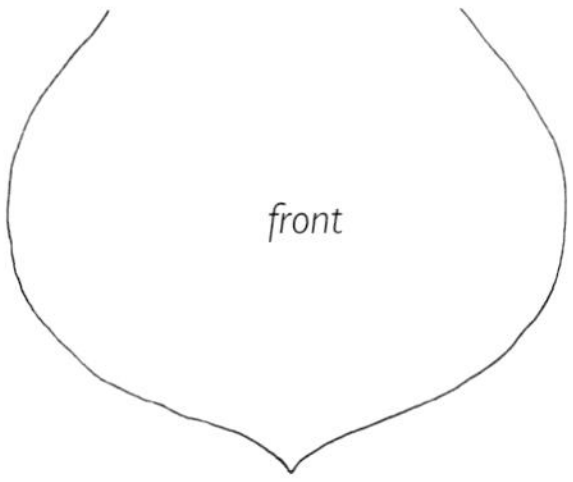

Diagram 2

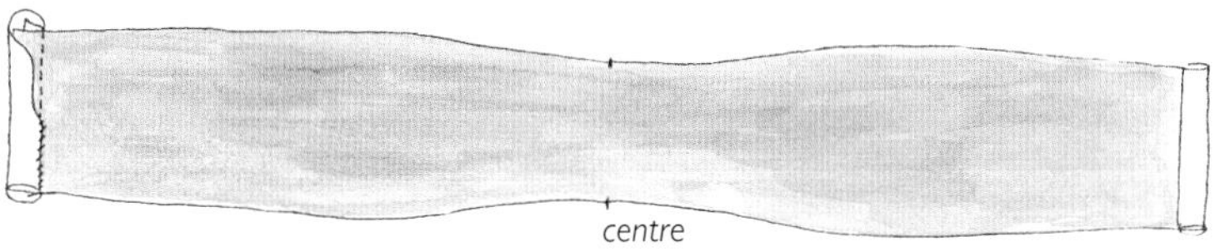

Diagram 3

2. Now work the embroidery for the front. Cut four pieces of silk, slightly larger than the front panel. Work cut-back appliqué (see diagram 4) and machine embroider curvy lines, as on the back panel, between the cut-back appliqué designs. Using Jap gold, couch down swirling lines (see page 121). Bond the embroidery to the front section of the pelmet Vilene (Pellon), carefully making sure the embroidery is protected with a pressing cloth. Trim off the excess silk around the edge of the Vilene. Bind the straight edge at the top of the front as shown in diagram 4.

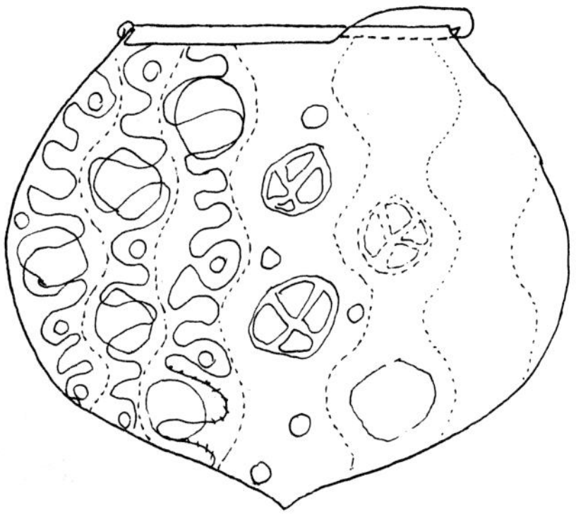
Diagram 4

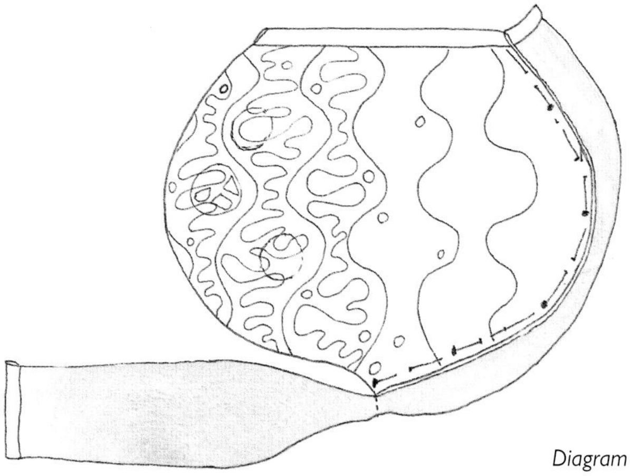
Diagram 5

3. Placing wrong sides together, pin the centre of the gusset to the centre of the lower edge of the front. Pin, tack (baste) and stitch the gusset to the front panel from the centre up each side (see diagram 5). Pin, tack (baste) and stitch the other side of the gusset to the back of the purse, matching centres and incorporating a loop at the centre of the flap. Trim the seam allowances evenly and bind all the edges using crossways binding (see page 103). Add small beads to the flap.

4. Add a tassel at the bottom, stitching the points of the back and the front panels together. The tassel illustrated is made from a piece of dyed and pleated silk that has been doubled over and bound with braid and then stitched to the purse. Small beads were added to the edges of the pleated silk to echo those on the flap.

5. Make a handle of the required length, using soft cord and a long strip of silk fabric (see page 109). Either stitch three or four beads in a row or one long bead across the gap between the front and the back panel on each side. Attach the handle by looping each end of the covered cord over the beads and secure by wrapping (see page 110). For further embellishment, wrap small sections of the cord handle at intervals with threads or ribbons.

Detail of gusseted purse

A canvaswork purse

The purse below has a multi-coloured effect achieved by using space-dyed yarn on a layered background. The purse measures 18cm (7in) from side to side in any direction. Two octagons were marked out and tacked (basted) on two pieces of canvas with 22 holes to the inch. Each canvas side was worked in the same way: torn or cut pieces of organza were arranged across the surface and tacked (basted) down. Some pieces overlapped but the canvas was still visible. Using space-dyed silk thread, an overall grid pattern was worked over the organza and through the canvas. When both sides were complete, a straight silk gusset was stitched to five sides of each octagon. The purse was lined with silk. For the fastening, two octagonal pieces of card with central square holes were worked with buttonhole stitch and attached to each side of the purse (see diagram 56, page 123). The machined-cord handle was doubled and looped through these and the ends joined and wrapped. The fastening, made from the same machined cord, was fashioned into a Turk's head knot. (For machined cords, see page 108.)

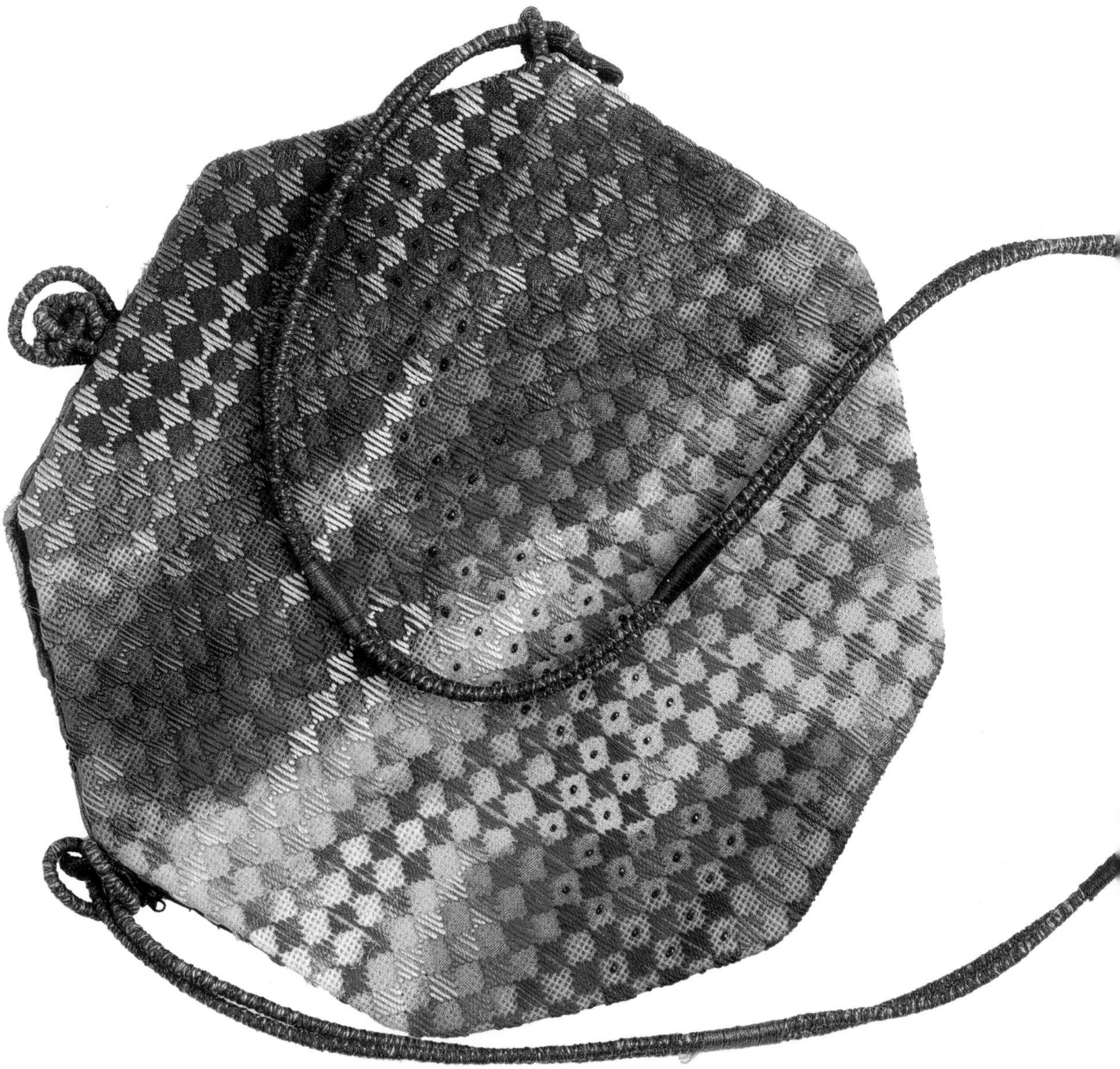

FRENCH BEADED PURSE
This French beaded purse from the 1920s is in excellent condition. The front and back sections are in one piece and have been entirely covered with beads. Two slightly gathered gussets have been let into the sides and the whole attached to a metal, enamelled frame, hinging at the sides. The frame has been further decorated with beads to match the rest of the purse. The inside is lined with cream satin and has three compartments, complete with a mirror and matching coin purse. A bead-covered strip is attached to the frame at the back to act as a small handle. A label inside states that it has been made in France.

CANVASWORK PURSE
The multi-coloured effect of this gusseted purse was achieved with space-dyed yarn on canvas layered with organzas (see page 120).

CHAPTER EIGHT DRAWSTRING PURSES

It was fashionable in both the mediaeval and Elizabethan eras to hang purses from girdles and belts. The drawstring was ideal for the purpose, offering both a means of suspension and of closure. However, drawstring purses existed long before the medieval period. Sinews, strips of leather, cords and ribbons have been passed through slits, holes, tabs and loops, all to achieve the same result, the security of valuables about the person.

The purses suspended from drawstrings vary enormously. The first money purses may very well have been circles of leather with holes punched around the perimeter and a strip of leather passed through the holes. Usually two cords are needed, each threaded in the opposite direction, to pull the purse closed. A knot at opposite sides allows easy opening.

Some purses have only one drawstring, which can be tied and wrapped around the neck of the purse. The purse shape can be square, like the 17th-century sweet purses or two-sided and cup-shaped like the incense purses from China.

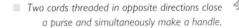

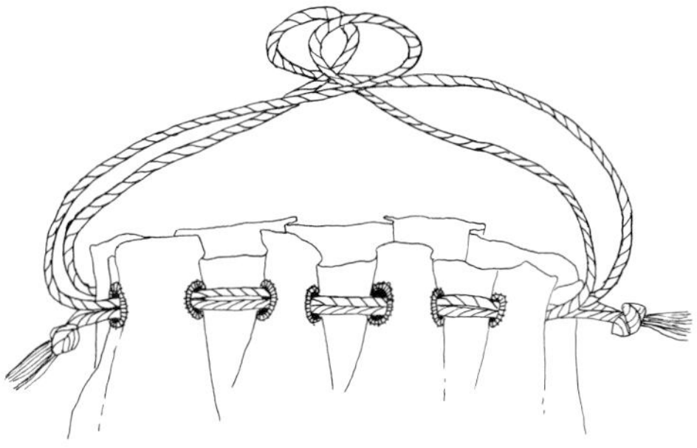

Two cords threaded in opposite directions close a purse and simultaneously make a handle.

MIE IWATSUBO'S PURSE
Mie Iwatsubo takes the idea of drawstring purses to a new plane by apparently having drawstrings throughout her purses. In this purse there is, however, only one functional drawstring, which operates on the inside pleats at the top of the purse. The others, made of felt string, are purely decorative. Mie calls her purses 'bulb bags'. They have a wonderfully organic feel to them, reminiscent of mushroom gills or seed pods. Using shibori techniques, Mie's hand-made felt is immersed in three separate dye baths to achieve the subtle colourings and to simultaneously set the pleats.

HARLEQUIN PURSE

This purse is not for the faint-hearted. English patchwork, worked over papers, was used in colours gleaned from the sleeve border shown on page 88. For instructions for this patchwork, see page 118.

Materials

- 20cm (8in) squares Habotai silk or cotton in 10 different colours
- 24 x 50cm (9 x 20in) black silk or cotton fabric
- 23 x 40cm (9 x 15in) lining fabric
- 20 x 34cm (8 x 13in) cotton wadding
- 1m (1yd) square thick tracing paper
- 2m (2¼ yd) cord
- Selection of coloured wires
- Selection of embroidery threads
- Black cotton thread for sewing
- 2 x 15cm (6in) long wool tops in two colours
- Strips of fabric in two colours, each 20cm (8in) long and 7.5cm (3in) wide

Method

1. To make the purse you will need 30 x 2.5cm (1in) squares of thick tracing paper or thin cartridge paper. Cut each of these squares diagonally to make 60 triangles. Accuracy is essential. Using the English patchwork technique, stitch triangles of Habotai silk or thin cotton together to form a strip of three rows of twenty triangles.

2. Next, add a border of plain fabric to each long side of the patchwork. Both borders must be the length of the patchwork plus a 1cm (⅜in) seam allowance at each short end. The top border must be 9cm (3½in) and the lower border 7cm (2¾in) wide. On each border, crease a seam allowance turning of 1cm (⅜in), using an iron, along one long side. Place the patchwork right sides together with the border, pin and oversew (see diagram 1). Carefully press the wrong side of the patchwork and both borders. Remove the papers from the patchwork except the three patches at each short end. These will help to keep the shape of the patchwork while the embroidery is worked.

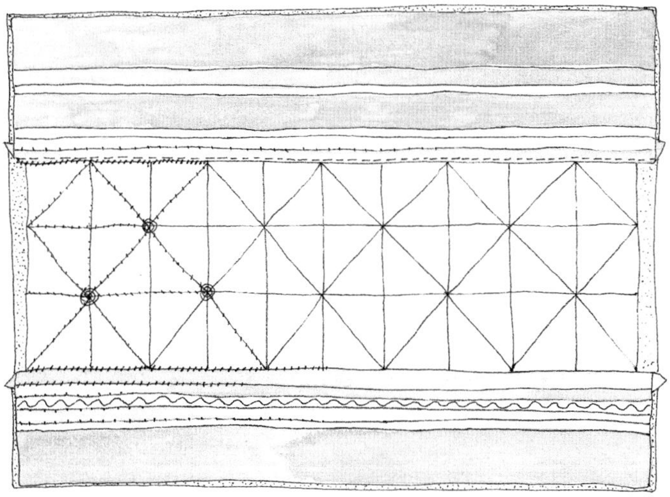

Diagram 1

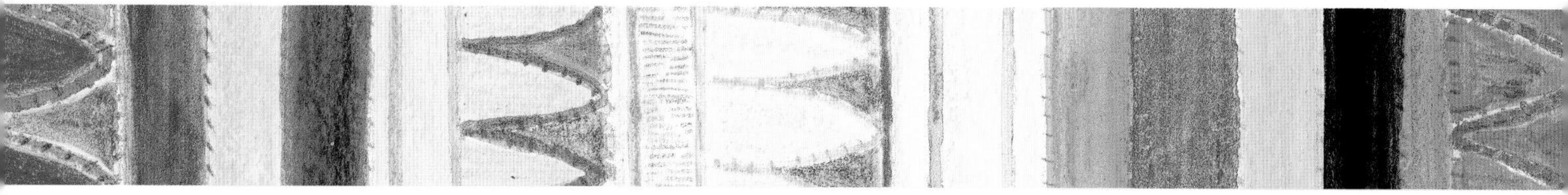

Drawing of a sleeve border from Thailand, which was the inspiration for the Harlequin Purse. The whole border is made of pieced strips of fabric, some decorated with applied triangles, couching and tiny rows of neat stitching.

3. Tack (baste) the patchwork to a piece of cotton wadding the same size. Spot-quilt the patchwork, using threads, beads or, as in the illustration, coloured wires. These were wound around a darning needle to make spirals and then couched down with sewing cotton. Next add lines of couching, strips of fabric rouleau or embroidery stitches to both borders.

4. Cut a piece of lining fabric the same size as the patchwork and borders. Next, make eight tabs for the drawstrings. Take the two strips of contrasting fabrics, fold with right sides together lengthways, and stitch a 1cm (⅜in) seam. Turn through and press. Cut each strip into four equal lengths. Fold each tab in half. Next lay the lining fabric with right side up. Arrange, pin and tack (baste) the tabs into place at regular intervals along the top edge (see diagram 2). Place the bordered patchwork on top, right side down, aligning the long edge of the lining with the long edge of the top border. Pin and machine stitch together along the long edge. Trim away any excess wadding in the seam allowance and press the seam lightly. Press a seam allowance along the lower border.

5. Next join the side seams. Iron a seam allowance on both short ends of both borders. Fold right sides together, matching the short sides. Trim and slipstitch the short edges of the wadding. Turn through and gently remove the last six papers. Pin and oversew the patchwork. Next, oversew the borders. Gather the bottom edge of the lower border, making sure the seam allowance is inside. Secure with several stitches.

Diagram 2

6. Thread two drawstrings through the tabs and add tassels (see page 117) to the ends and on opposite sides.

Sketchbook page of designs based on the drawing opposite, which resulted in the idea of pieced triangles incorporating couched threads and coloured wire.

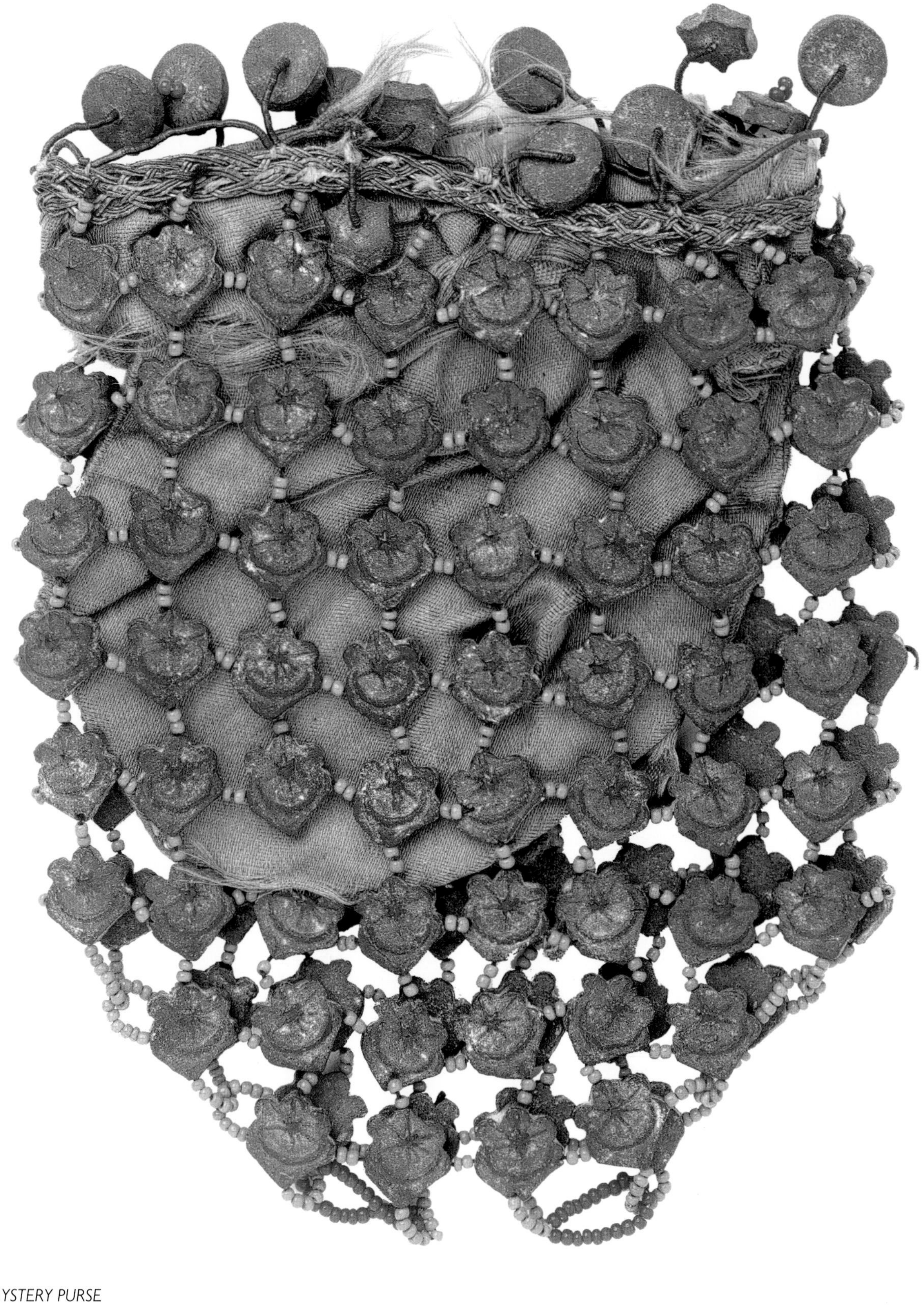

MYSTERY PURSE

This small, drawstring purse is something of a mystery. Only 9cm (3½in) long and 7.5cm (3in) wide, it is lined with fragile blue silk. The beads look like pressed lead, but they are not heavy enough. They appear to have a star and crescent impressed on them. They are strung together in a chequerboard fashion, spaced with tiny pink beads, the thread passing horizontally through the pressed beads. Similar purses were made in 1810 in France, often displaying motifs from Egypt to commemorate Napoleon's expedition there in 1798, and this is almost certainly an example of one. The two loops of beads at the base of the purse seem to indicate a lost tassel.

SPACE-DYED LACE PURSE

This purse has been made from a sample, worked previously, of space-dyed strips of lace borders. These were cut into squares and hand-stitched to a wadded silk background. Quilting and beading further enhance the surface. Silk, which had been previously pleated and hand-dyed, has been used for the lining and for a band across the top of the purse, as well as two narrow folded strips of contrasting silk in yellow and dark grey. The construction method was the same as for the slashed velvet purse on page 52. Buttonhole bars (see page 121) hold the drawstring, which has been made of rouleau. A Thai border (see page 107) has been inserted along the lower edge of the purse and on the rouleau drawstring. The joins in the rouleau were wrapped with silk thread (see page 110).

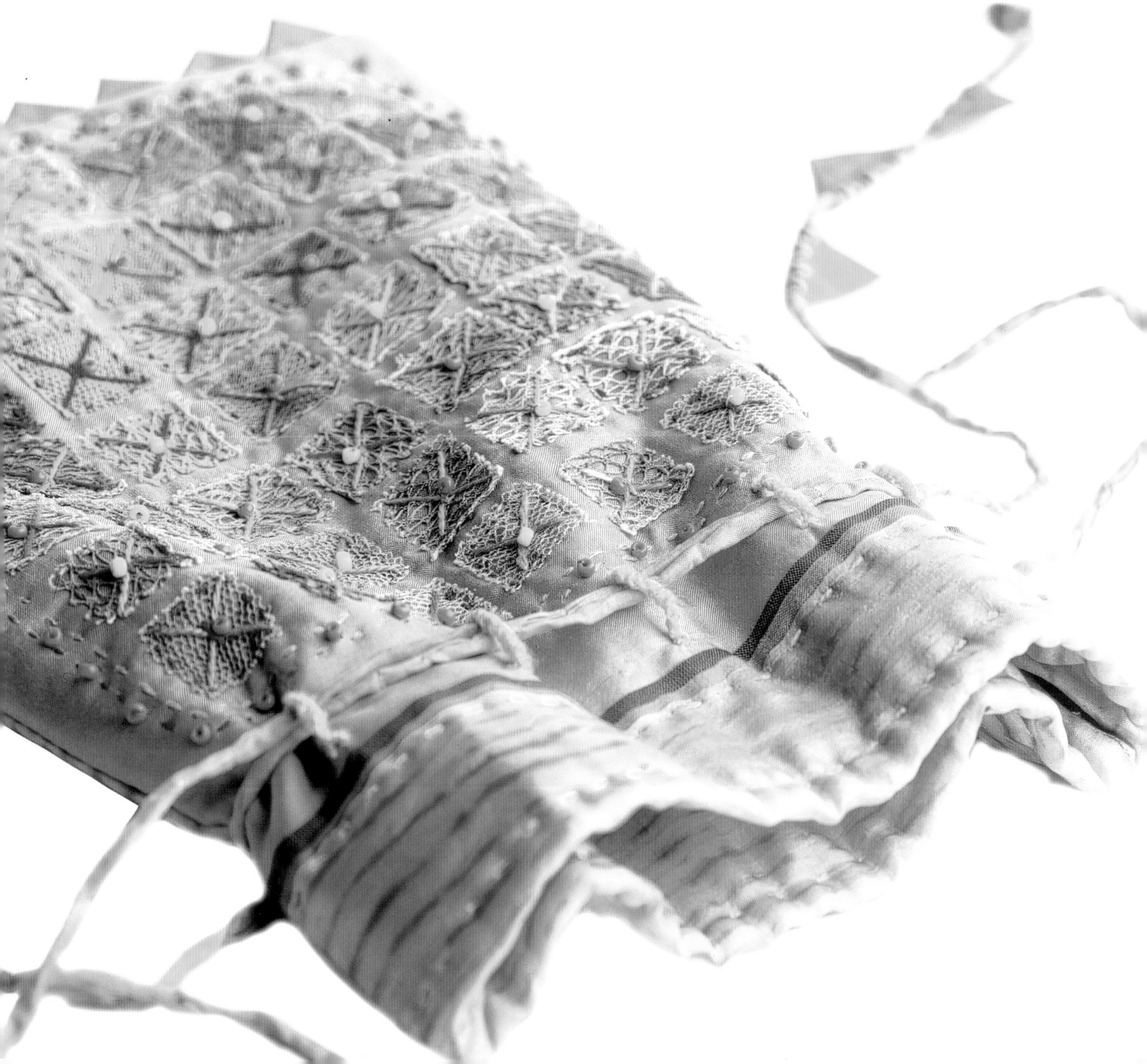

CHAPTER NINE BOX PURSES

As the name implies, box purses have stiff bases and, in some cases, rigid sides. Naturally, the shape of the purse depends on the height of the sides and the shape of the base, but whatever their dimensions, box purses have a sculptural feel about them.

Cubes, pyramids, cylinders and tower shapes are all possible. The architectural qualities of hard edges and clean lines can be used to great effect. Box purses might even appear monumental.

Box purses can be more complicated in their construction than the other purses described so far. A purse with a square base will have more sides, after all, but this could also be regarded as a wonderful opportunity for more decoration on an increased area. It is always worth spending time making a card mock-up first. The shape of the purse below, for instance, was only achieved after several attempts at manipulating both the shape of the elliptical base and the curved sides.

TWO-SIDED PURSE WITH A CURVED BASE
This purse was based on a triangular-shaped ceramic dish. The sides were gently curved and the corners were rounded. Using this shape, two identical sides were completed, with one corner on each turned down. An elliptical base was stiffened, covered and bound, then stitched to one curved edge of each side of the purse. The handle was made with cord covered with striped silk and attached to the outsides. Flat, folded bands of silk were stitched at intervals around the handle.

EMILY JO GIBBS'S SHELL BUCKET PURSE
This whimsical seaside purse was made by Emily Jo Gibbs. Emily has made a sterling silver frame and handle to which a stiffened base of red duchesse satin has been attached.The satin is hand embroidered with gently swimming fish and scallop shells. Unusually for a purse with stiffened sides, there is a drawstring top which is made of crepe-backed satin. The entire surface of the top is covered with hand-made copper and silver sea-shells and starfish, all made by Emily.

PURSE BASED ON A TURKISH TEXTILE

The purse illustrated here was inspired by a textile, thought to be a ewer cover, from the Grand Bazaar in Istanbul (see page 96). With the sides raised around the central square and stitched together, a cube without a top can be formed. The diamond chequerboard arrangement of free-floating patchwork pieces, stitched together at their corners, was the inspiration for the decoration on the purse.

Materials

- 50 x 15cm (20 x 6in) black felt
- 50 x 75cm (20 x 30in) silk fabric for stiffened squares
- 50 x 92cm (20 x 36in) stripped silk
- 60 x 50cm (24 x 20in) lining fabric
- 35cm x 2cm (14 x ¾in) strip Bondaweb (Wonder-Under)
- 42 x 10cm (17 x 4in) stiff card
- Scraps of organza
- PVA glue
- Craft glue
- Gold and blue acrylic paint
- 5 wooden skewers
- 200 small beads
- Blue embroidery thread
- 1m (40in) Russia braid or something similar
- 30 x 50cm (12 x 20in) cotton wadding

Diagram 2

Method

1. Cut a strip of black felt measuring 35 x 11cm (13¾ x 4⅜in). On the felt, mark out a rectangle measuring 32 x 8cm (12⅝ x 3⅛in) with a seam allowance of 1.5cm (⅝in) all around. Mark out four 8cm (3⅛in) squares in the rectangle, using a sliver of soap (see diagram 1).

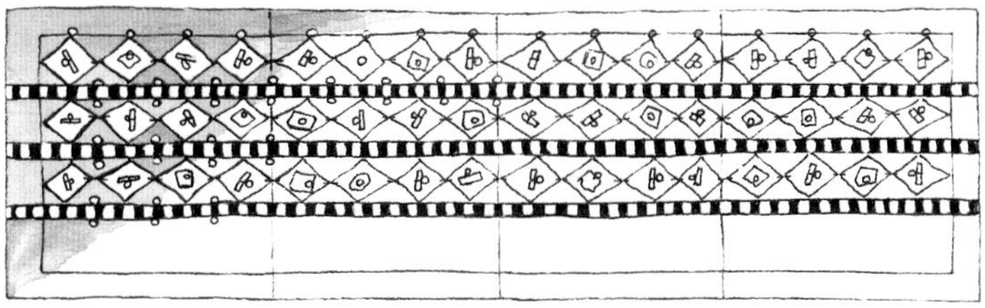

Diagram 1

2. Iron Bondaweb (Wonder-Under) to the reverse of a piece of striped silk measuring 35 x 2cm (13¾ x ¾in). Cut three strips, each 5mm (3/16in) wide, using a steel rule and a rotary cutter. Peel off the paper backing and iron each strip to the felt, making three parallel lines at 1.5cm (⅝in) intervals (see diagram 1).

3. Make 60 stiffened silk squares (see page 115), each measuring 1.5cm (⅝in). Decorate with beads, sequins, painted sections of wooden skewers, small scraps of organza or combinations of these. Stitch the squares at the corners between the bonded silk strips, four between each 8cm (3⅛in) marking, leaving the squares at the end of the strip free. Anchor the three bonded silk strips by stitching beads at intervals along their lengths (see diagram 1).

4. To make the base, cut an 8cm (3⅛in) square of stiff card and cover with black felt, either with glue or by hand stitching. Make a piece of rouleau (see page 103) with a strip of silk measuring 33 x 2cm (13 x ¾in). Slipstitch around the edge of the base, easing around the corners and dovetailing the ends (see diagram 2).

A textile design from Istanbul, thought to be a ewer cover, in pieced, worn cotton fabrics. The diamond shapes in each quarter are joined at their corners and 'free-float' within the patched triangle borders.

5. To make the sides, cut a strip of mounting board or other stiff card measuring 32 x 8cm ($12^1/_2$ x $3^1/_8$in). Score it vertically every 8cm ($3^1/_8$in). Pin the embroidered strip to the card, matching the scores in the card with the 8cm ($3^1/_8$ in) markings on the felt. Turn 1.5cm ($^5/_8$ in) of felt to the wrong side all round and glue, cutting the excess from the corners, as shown in diagram 3.

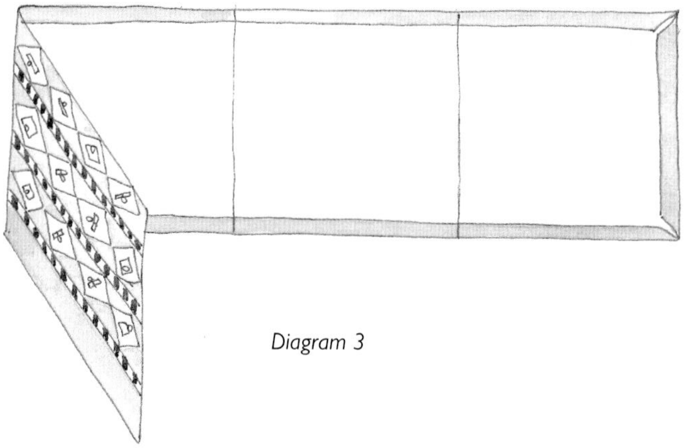

Diagram 3

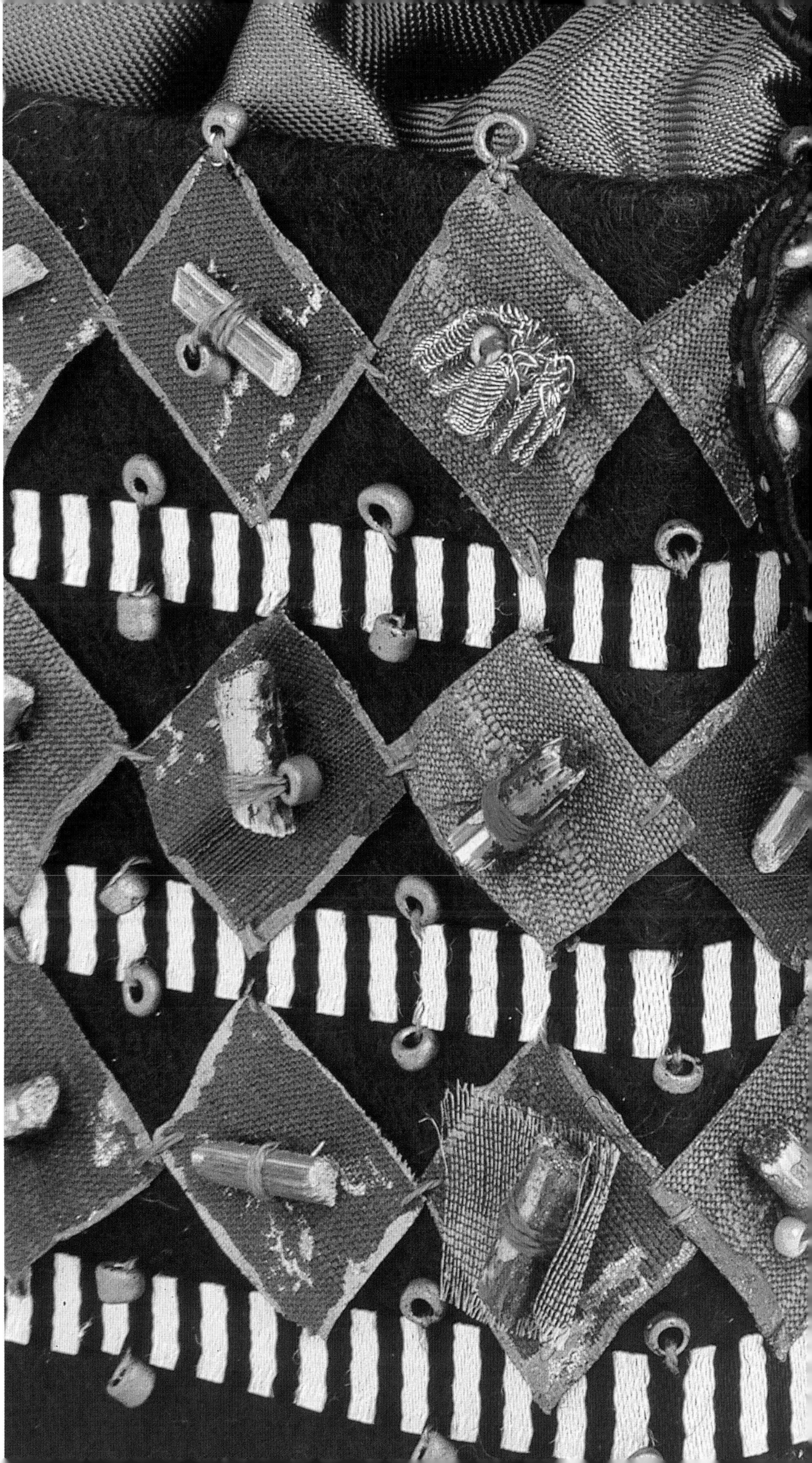

Detail of Box Purse.

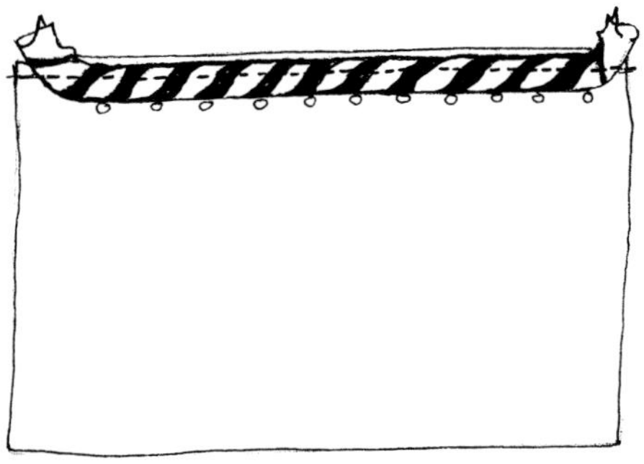

Diagram 4

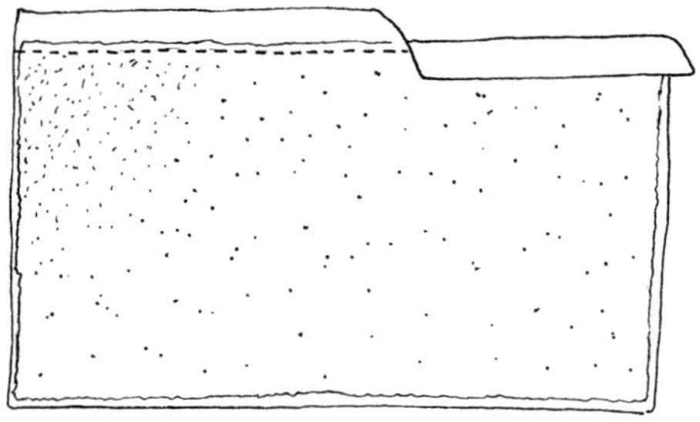

Diagram 5

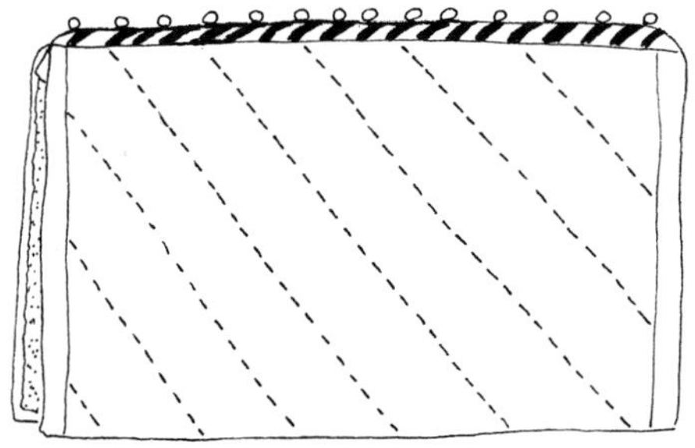

Diagram 6

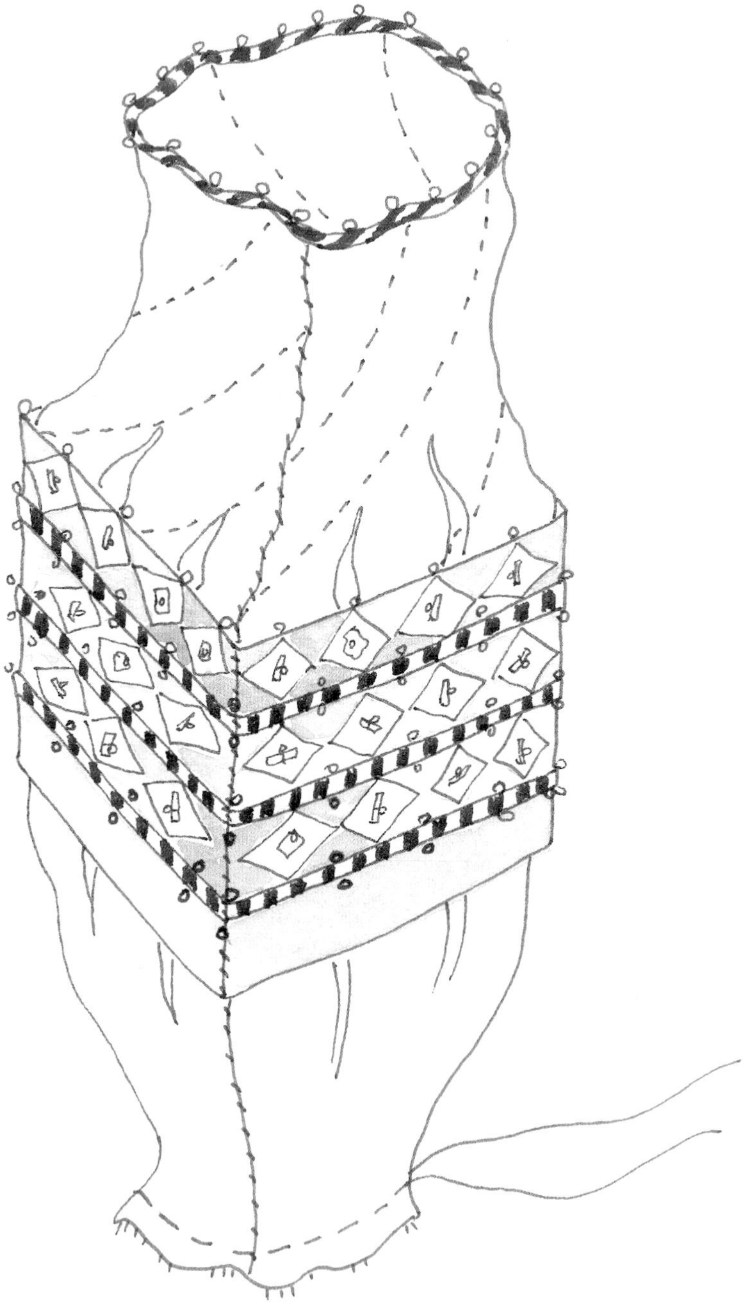

Diagram 7

6. Now cut two pieces of silk and one piece of cotton wadding, each 48 x 25cm (19 x 10in). Make a further piece of rouleau, 45cm (17¾in) long, using a 2cm (¾in) wide strip of the striped silk. Stitch the rouleau to the long side of one of the pieces of silk, leaving a 1cm (⅜ in) edge, matching the raw edges and tapering the rouleau off at both ends (see diagram 4). Stitch beads at intervals along the top edge of the rouleau. Machine the cotton wadding along one long edge of the other piece of silk, 1cm (⅜in) from the edge. Trim away excess wadding and turn the seam allowance of silk over to the wrong side, as shown in diagram 5. Slipstitch the wadded silk piece to the other side of the rouleau. Mark a 1cm (⅜in) seam allowance line with a sliver of soap on both short ends. Quilt lines diagonally through all layers from the rouleau to the raw edges, avoiding the seam allowances (see diagram 6). Trim the wadding from the seam allowances and turn them in. Slipstitch the seams to form a tube. Run a gathering thread around the lower edge of the tube, opposite the rouleau, and leave the threads free.

7. Fold the stiffened, decorated felt piece and slipstitch the two short ends together. Anchor the last of the stiffened silk squares at the finished seam. Feed the quilted tube through into the stiffened felt piece leaving 9cm (3½in) above the top edge of the felt. Stitch at intervals along the top edge, gathering slightly (see diagram 7). Pull up the gathering thread around the bottom edge of the tube and secure the ends, leaving the raw edges of the silk facing down. Oversew the base to the sides, covering the gathered raw edges inside.

8. To make the cord and tassels, decorate a 1m (39in) length of Russia braid with stitching and beads. Stitch six squares of stiffened, decorated silk together to form a cube. Thread the Russia braid through and make a knot to secure. Finish with a twisted tassel (see page 116). Repeat for the other end of the braid. Wrap the braid around the quilted silk top and tie.

Other box purses

A PURSE WITH CARD AND WOOD

Box-style purses can be made with various shapes of base. The velvet purse seen here has a diamond-shaped base, which has been stiffened with card. Deep red velvet and electric blue silk were chosen as contrasting colours for this purse. The velvet sides were worked in a strip before being attached to the base. The card plaque and wooden skewer embellishments seen on this purse are described on page 111. Other decorations include machining on velvet with metallic thread. In this purse, the draping qualities of the velvet were sacrificed by tacking (basting) the velvet to pelmet Vilene in order to provide a good, solid base for the machining. To allow the machine embroidery to show, it is necessary to machine back and forth several times in more or less the same place until the deep fabric pile is flattened.

An extra deep-blue lining was added – see diagram below – so that a little would show above the top edge. The purse was finished with strips of gathered silk tissue and beads along the top and bottom edges. A shaped, lined handle was attached inside the rim.

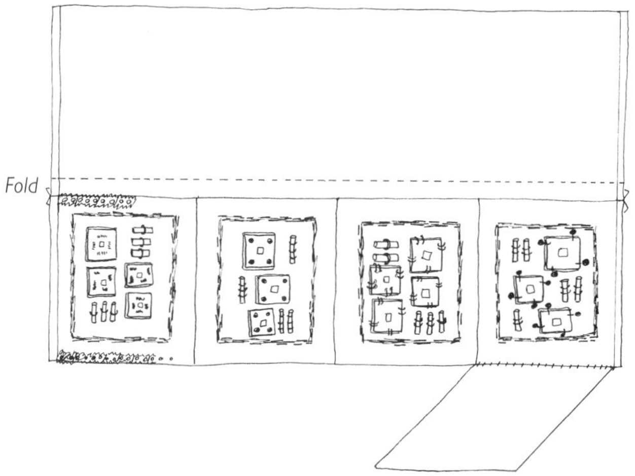

Plan for the four sides of the purse, the lining, seamed at the top edge, and the diamond-shaped base.

A PURSE WITH SLASHED VELVET

This slashed-velvet purse has a circular base and a slashed-velvet body, supported by a wadded lining. A strip of velvet was printed with gold fabric paints and slashed and tied diagonally at intervals (see page 106). It was further decorated with beads and plaques. The top was gathered horizontally and tied at intervals with ribbons. This gave the top edge more body. The whole velvet strip was then stitched to green silk, which can be seen through the slashing. A quilted silk inner purse was made, slightly taller than the velvet, in order to show above the top edge. The base was made of silk-covered card, attached to the seamed velvet body. The inner purse was positioned inside, and secured at intervals to the velvet. A matching, lined handle and tab were attached between the velvet and the silk inner purse and stitched to both. Finally, a spiral of ribbon-covered wire (see page 110) was stitched around the base to add stability.

CHAPTER TEN FINISHES AND DECORATIONS

The quality of the finishing details on a purse is so important that it is well worth spending time and effort perfecting these techniques. There are several processes common to many of the purses in this book which, once mastered, can be used time and again in many different guises.

Basic skills

Making crossways strips

Crossways strips can be used for binding the edges of purses, for making rouleaux, and for incorporating in tassels and handles. Any flexible material can be used as long as it doesn't fray too much. Start by cutting strips of fabric, 3–4cm ($1^1/_4$–$1^1/_2$in) wide, at 45 degrees to the selvage. These must be accurately cut. To join several lengths, place the ends of the two strips at right angles to each other and stitch with the grain of the fabric. Press the seam open and trim (see diagrams 1 and 2.)

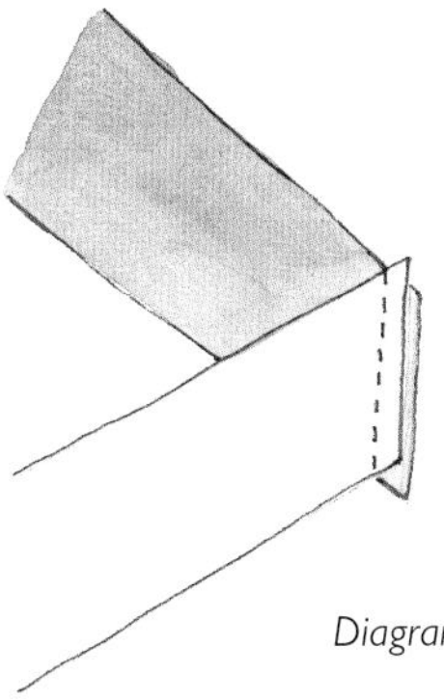

Diagram 1

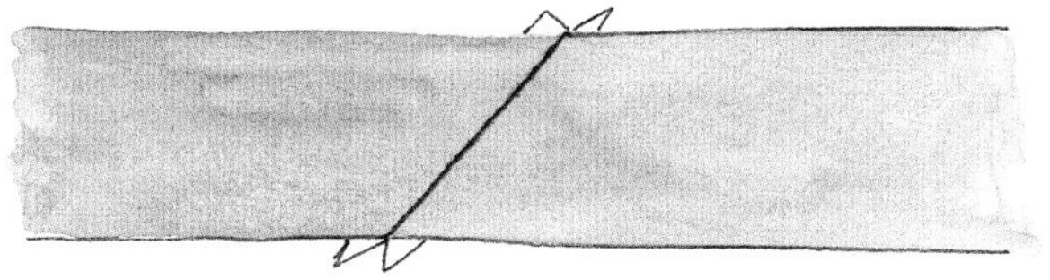

Diagram 2

Rouleaux

To make a rouleau, take a crossways-cut strip of the required length and stitch along the folded fabric, right sides together. Trim any surplus seam allowance. Place a bodkin or blunt needle inside and stitch the eye to the end of the fabric, as shown in diagram 3. Pass the needle back through the tube, feeding the fabric in, until the rouleau is completely turned through (see diagram 4).

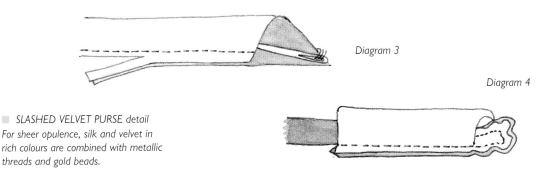

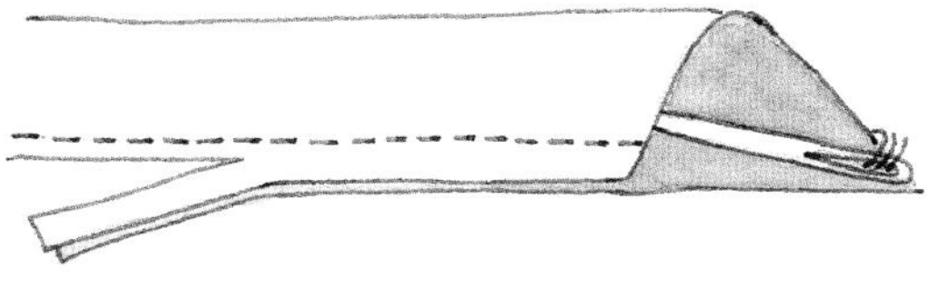

Diagram 3

Diagram 4

SLASHED VELVET PURSE detail
For sheer opulence, silk and velvet in rich colours are combined with metallic threads and gold beads.

Bound edges

A binding made from a matching or contrasting fabric is one of the simplest and neatest ways to finish the edges of your purse. A crossways strip, folded lengthways, is stitched around the front edge of the purse, with raw edges aligned as shown in diagram 5. Next, fold the strip over to the wrong side and pin in place. Because the folded binding is on the cross of the fabric, it will smooth over the edge in a beautifully neat manner and can be slipstitched in place with ease.

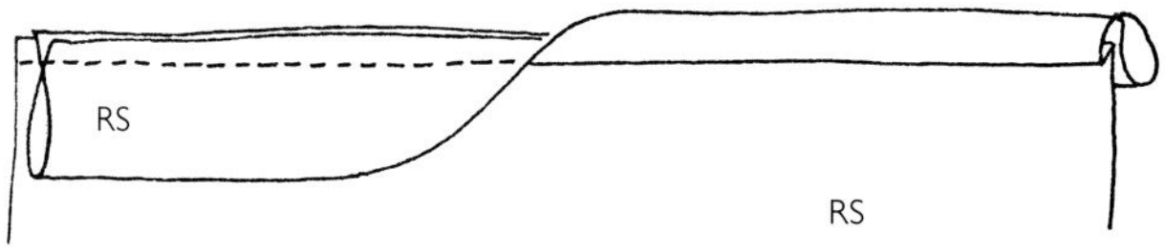

Diagram 5

Using Bondaweb (Wonder-Under)

Bondaweb is an adhesive web attached to greaseproof paper. It is used to bond fabrics together when ironed. Follow the manufacturer's instructions, and, in addition, cover both the ironing board and the work with greaseproof paper or baking parchment in order to avoid sticky surfaces that could burn onto the iron.

When producing a large amount of bonded appliqué work, several pieces of fabric can be ironed with Bondaweb in preparation. The images can then be drawn freehand on the paper backing, remembering that they will be reversed when bonded to the fabric. Alternatively, the paper backing can be used to trace outlines, roughly cut out and ironed onto the fabric. Because the paper-backed Bondaweb stiffens the fabric, more intricate shapes can then be cut out without fraying. This is especially helpful when using thin materials, such as Habotai silk.

Bonding silk to velvet

Sumptuous effects can result when rich materials of differing weights are bonded together, and then cut. If velvet and silk are bonded together, the thickness of the velvet will support the silk when cut and folded back. The silk will thus keep its rounded shape, displaying its natural lustre to best advantage. When bonding silk to velvet, iron the Bondaweb to the silk first; remove the paper backing, and gently iron the bonded fabric to the reverse of the velvet, avoiding crushing the pile. Some gentle steam may be necessary.

Diagram 6

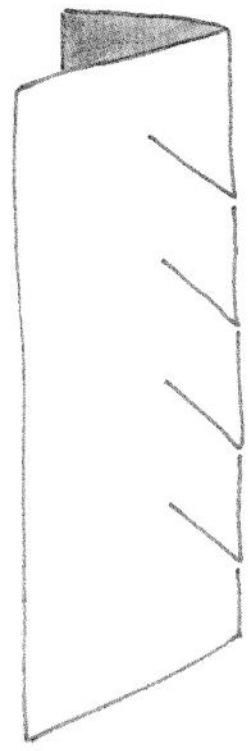

Diagram 7

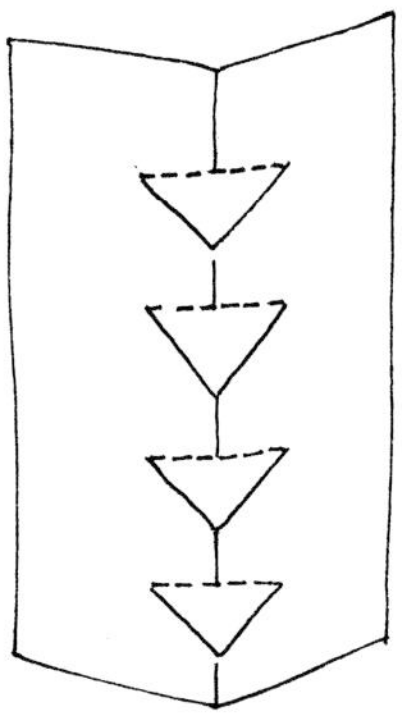

Diagram 8

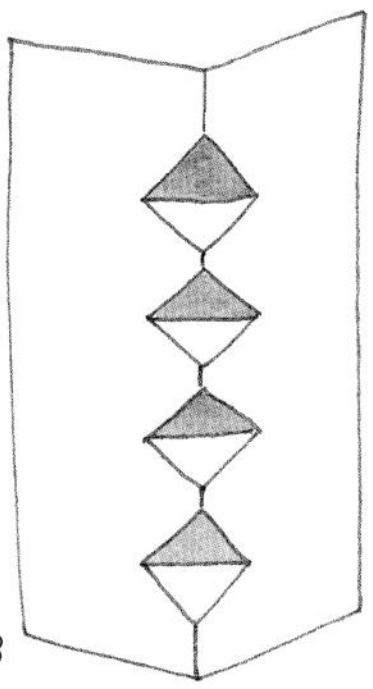

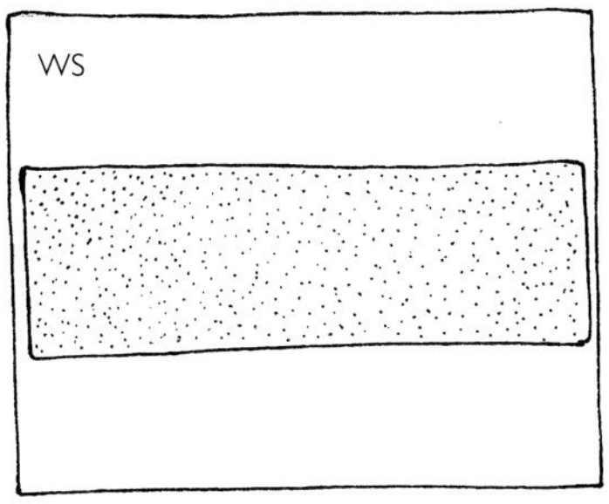

Diagram 9

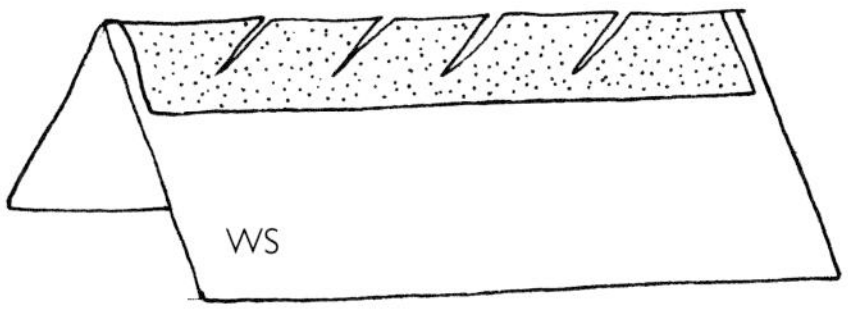

Diagram 10

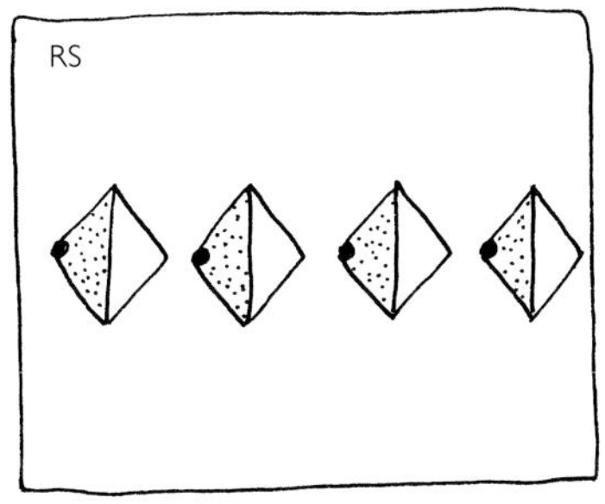

Diagram 11

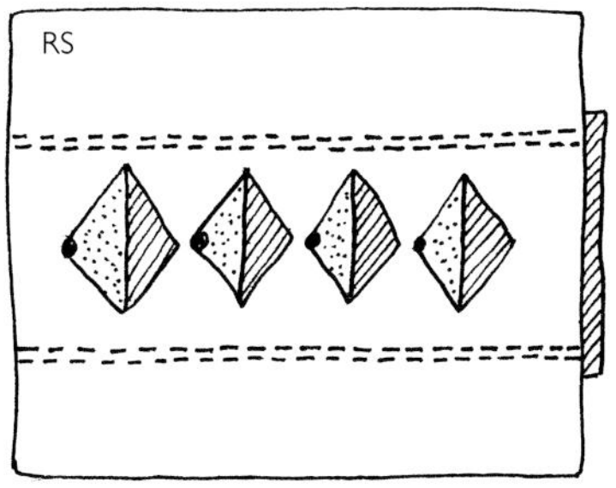

Diagram 12

Cutting bonded silk and velvet

Before cutting into bonded fabrics, it is advisable to try out some ideas on paper. Take a strip of paper, say 10 x 30cm (4 x 12in). Fold it in half lengthways and make slanting cuts into the fold (see diagram 6). Flatten the paper out, and fold the resulting triangular flaps back (see diagrams 7 and 8). Experiment with other strips of paper, making the cuts closer together or further apart, or more or less slanting. Each variation will give a different effect.

Now for the fabrics. To make a strip of bonded and cut silk and velvet, as seen in the purse on page 54, take a strip of velvet and a strip of silk the same length, but a third of the width of the velvet. Bond the silk to the velvet, as shown in diagram 9. Fold the bonded fabrics along the centre of the silk, mark at regular intervals with a sliver of soap and make slanting cuts (see diagram 10). Flatten out and gently fold back the cut fabrics, to reveal the silk. Secure with a stitch or a bead (see diagram 11). Repeat for all other cuts. Place a strip of silk of a contrasting colour under the cuts and secure with running stitches or further embroidery, as shown in diagram 12. More rows of cuts and folds could be added, along with further embellishments.

Slashing and tying velvet

To make a length of slashed-and-tied velvet suitable for the purse on page 52, you will need a rotary cutter, a cutting board, sharp embroidery scissors, a selection of narrow ribbons, and some beads and sequins. Take a piece each of silk and velvet, say 20 x 40cm (8 x 16in). Mark two pairs of parallel lines about 5cm (2in) apart across the back of the velvet with a sliver of soap (see diagram 13). With a rotary cutter, carefully make a number of diagonal slashes in three rows, between the soap lines (see diagram 14). Now place the silk under the velvet and stitch by hand or by machine between the rows of slashes and around the edges to stabilize the whole piece, as shown in diagram 15. Tie pairs of slashed edges together by slipping the ribbon, braid or thread under the first two slashes and tying tightly. If you roll the cut edges of velvet under as you tie the ribbon, any slight fraying will be concealed. After tying, cut the ends of the ribbon about 3cm (1¼in) long for further decoration. Continue along the rows, tying pairs as shown in diagram 16.

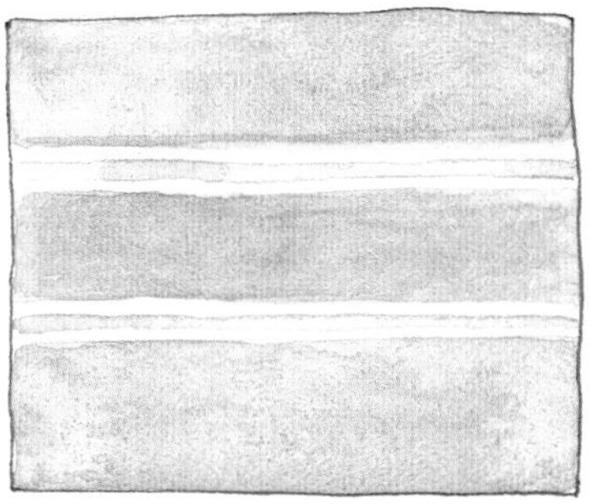

Diagram 13

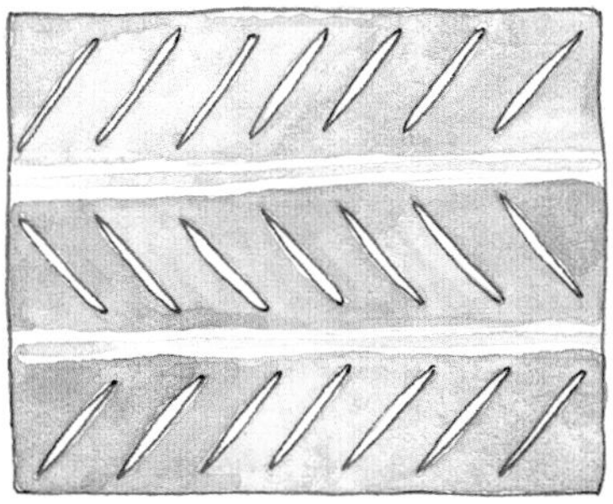

Diagram 14

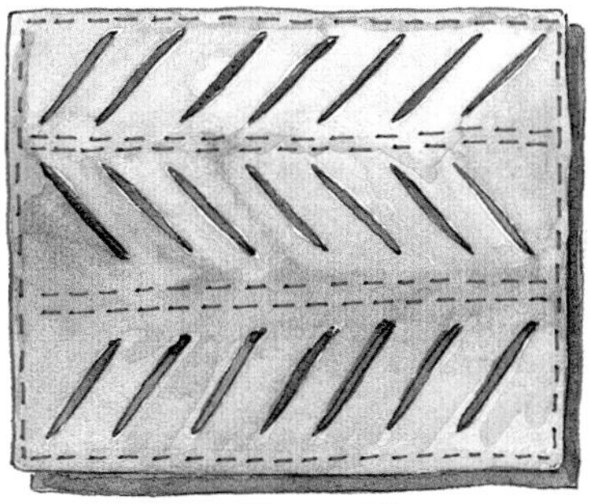

Diagram 15

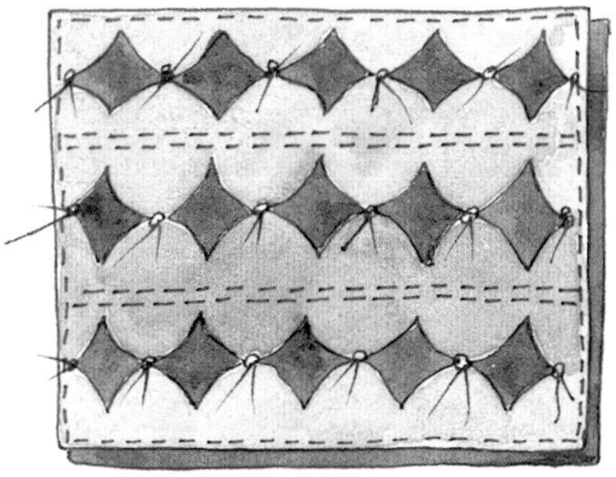

Diagram 16

Borders

Thai borders

To make folded points like the traditional ones made in Thailand, take a piece of cotton or silk fabric, 5cm (2in) square, and fold diagonally twice (see diagram 17). Repeat with another identical square and slip the first triangle into the second, as shown in diagram 17. Continue with further folded squares of fabric, slipping each into the last, to form a border. Pin, tack (baste) and stitch to a base fabric and cover raw edges with a strip of fabric. Alternatively, incorporate within a seam, with the points extending beyond the edge, as in the purse on page 91.

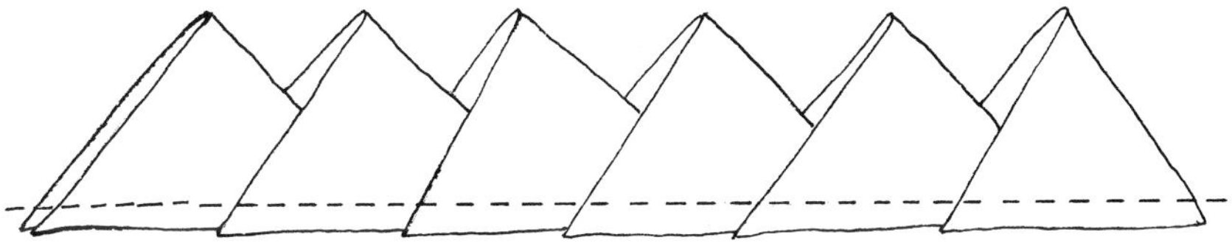

Diagram 18

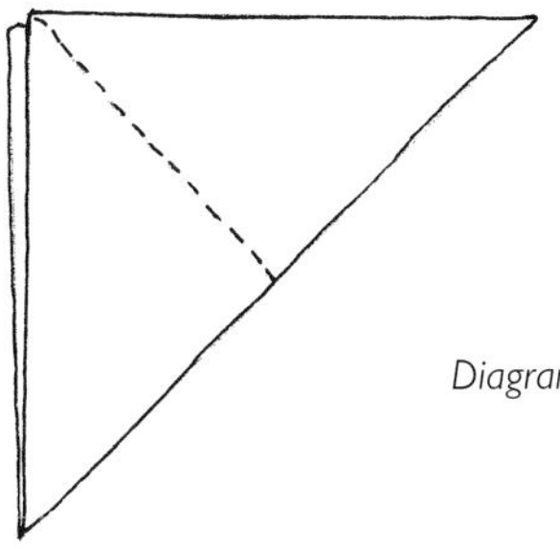

Diagram 17

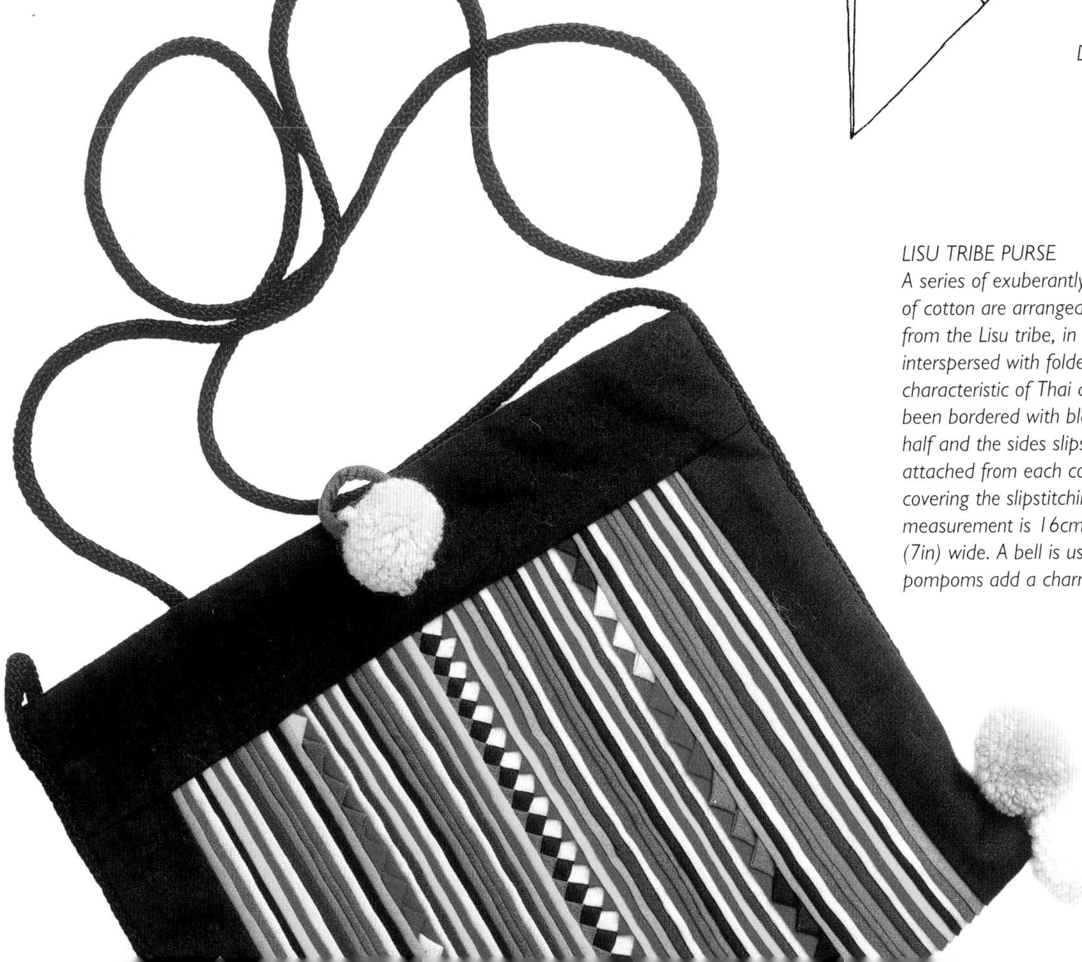

LISU TRIBE PURSE
A series of exuberantly coloured, folded strips of cotton are arranged on a long strip in this purse from the Lisu tribe, in Thailand. These have been interspersed with folded points, a technique characteristic of Thai decoration. The strip has been bordered with black cotton and folded in half and the sides slipstitched. The handle is attached from each corner and up the two sides, covering the slipstitching. The overall measurement is 16cm (6½in) long and 18cm (7in) wide. A bell is used for a fastening and wool pompoms add a charming finishing touch.

A pointed, bonded border

To make a border of the type shown on the tassel sampler on page 114, take a piece of closely woven fabric, such as cotton or the heavier weight Habotai silk, with Bondaweb (Wonder-Under) ironed on the reverse. Cut into strips of the required length by 2cm (3/4in) wide. On the paper backing, mark every 1.5cm (5/8in) along the length and make cuts 1.5cm (5/8in) deep at alternate marks (see diagram 19). Peel the paper backing off and fold the cut edges back to make a pointed border. As you work, touch each point with the tip of a warm iron to secure it.

For different effects try experimenting with a strip of paper, varying the spaces between the cuts and the depths of the cuts.

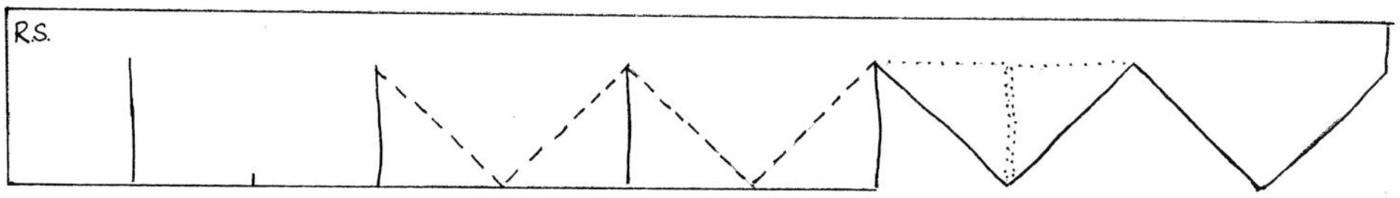

Diagram 19

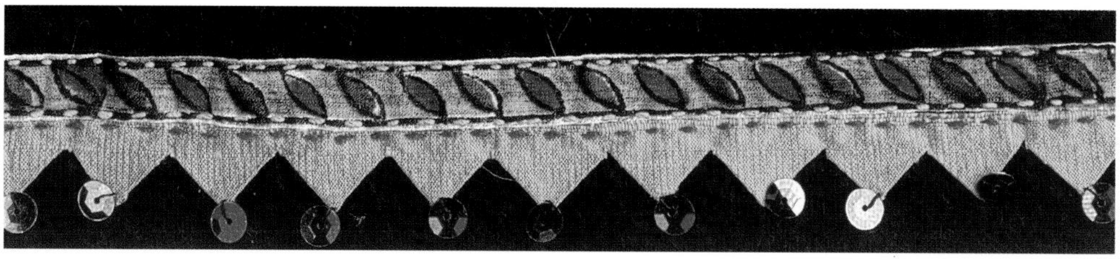

Cords and handles

Machined-cord handles

The core of these handles can be string, knitting yarn or nylon twine – in fact, any twine narrower than the zigzag stitch on your machine. The stiffer types of string will produce rounder cords. First cut some string the length of the required handle plus a little extra, for attachment to the purse. Set the zigzag stitch to the same width as your string and choose a short stitch length. Use machine embroidery threads or silk on both spool and bobbin. Now, zigzag from one end to the other, keeping the cord fairly taut. Several journeys may be needed to cover the string, giving the added opportunity to mix colours of thread to match or contrast with your purse, as on page 82.

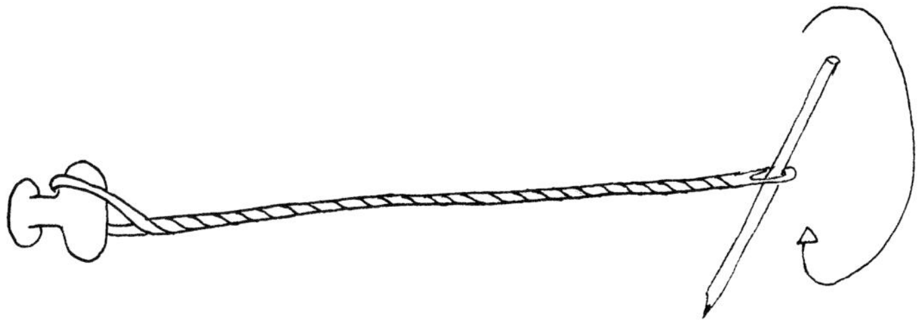

Diagram 20

Diagram 21

Twisted cords

Several lengths of machined cord can be twisted together or a number of yarns, cords or threads of differing thicknesses can be mixed. Group your chosen selection, and cut them three times the required length. Make a loop at each end, passing one over a hook or a door handle to anchor it and the other over a pencil, as shown in diagram 20. Keeping the threads taut, twist the pencil until the twist begins to turn on itself. Put your finger in the middle of the cords and take the pencil to the door handle. The cord will twist up on itself, as shown in diagram 21. Unhook the cord and it is ready for use.

Bound cords

Cording can be covered with the fabric used in your purse to make a matching handle. Cut a length of fabric slightly longer than the desired handle and a length of cord twice as long as the fabric. The fabric should be wide enough to wrap around the cord plus seam allowances. Fold the fabric in half, lengthways around the cord, with right sides inwards, aligning the cord and fabric at one end. Sew along the cord, stitching through the fabric only. Stitch across the end with the extra cord protruding, as shown in diagram 22. Trim off the seam allowances and pull the cord through, slipping the fabric over the extra cord (see diagram 23).

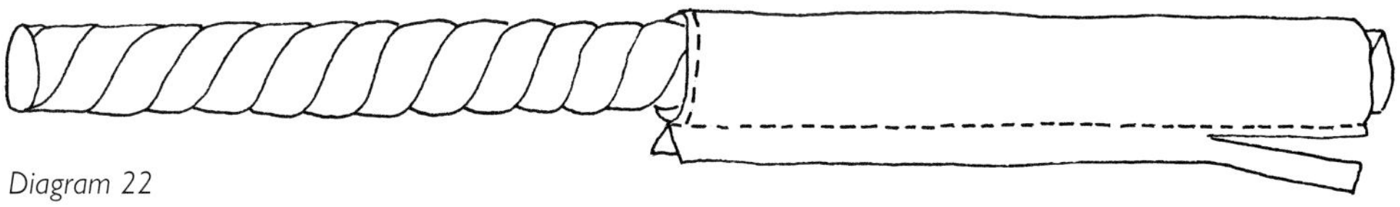

Diagram 22

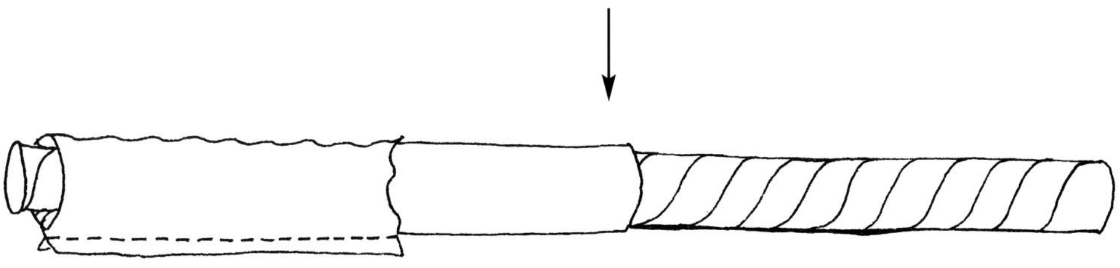

Diagram 23

Spiralled, wire-covered cord

The purse on page 101 has a spiral of space-dyed cord around the base. The cord strengthens the construction and adds a decorative edge. To make a similar arrangement, you will require garden wire, cut three times the required length, and tubular braid or ribbon. Bend the tip of the wire over to make it smooth enough to pass down the hollow braid. Now wind this around a wooden skewer or a knitting needle to make a spiral. Gently remove the stick. The resulting spiral can be over-stitched to the purse.

Wrapped cords

To wrap a cord or a skein of threads, take a length of thread and make a loop 5cm (2in) from one end, leaving a free end. Lay the loop along the cord to be wrapped and wind the thread around the cord and towards the loop. Pass the end of the thread through the loop and pull the free end so the thread disappears under the wrapped section, as in diagram 24.

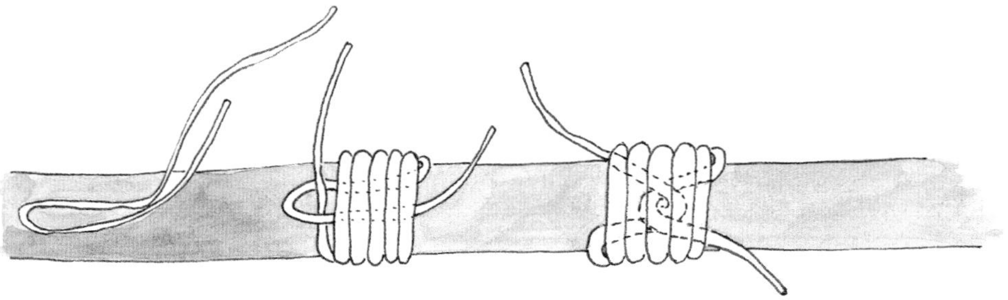

Diagram 24

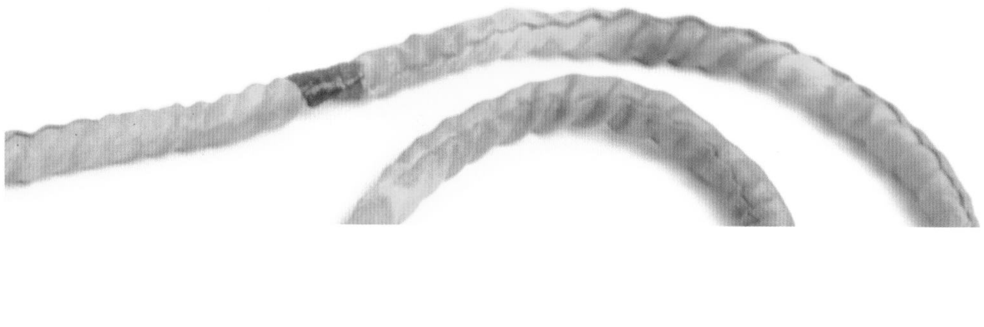

Embellishments

Decorated card plaques

The plaques stitched to the purse on page 100 are made with mounting board, but any stiff card could be used. Depending on the number and size needed, a sheet of card is pasted with glue, and a colour photocopy, a page from a sketchbook or a colourful magazine is stuck down. When it is dry, paint the surface with watered down PVA or varnish. Again, when this has dried, cut the card into squares and dip the edges in metallic paint, using a pair of tweezers to hold the pieces. For further effects, layers of paper can be built up before varnishing. Make holes with a stiletto or large needle before sewing the plaques to fabric (see diagram 25).

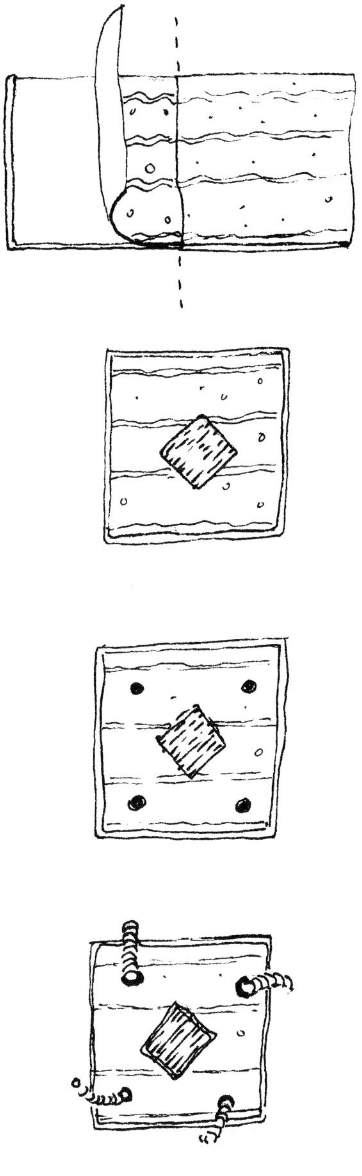

Diagram 25

Wooden skewers

Wooden skewers, of the type used for barbecue kebabs, can be painted, inked, or rolled in glued tissue paper or glitter before being cut up with wire cutters or a craft knife. A tiny spot of PVA glue under each piece of wooden skewer will hold it in place before it is stitched down.

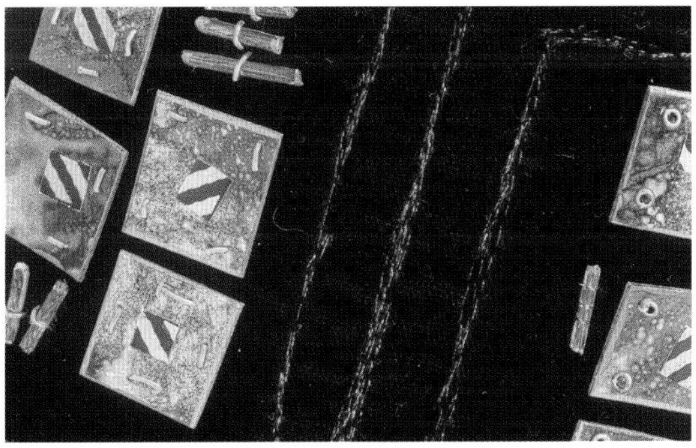

Stitching down beads

Most embroiderers are magpies where beads are concerned. Indeed it is not until you have accumulated a fair-sized collection that you can be confident of having exactly the right beads at your fingertips. I have been known to take a half-finished purse with me everywhere in case I should find a matching bead. I have also been known to buy a superb example and design a purse specifically for it. It is worth looking for bead necklaces in markets, both here and abroad, as these can yield unusual examples when dismantled.

The way in which beads are stitched down can also be important. For sheer opulence, they can be used in piles rather than singly, as in the first column of stitched beads in the bead sampler. Choose three or four sequins, ranging in size, and a small bead. Bring the needle up through the sequins, which are arranged in decreasing sizes, and then up through the bead. Take the thread over the bead and down through the sequins (see diagram 26). Secure on the reverse of the fabric. As can be seen, hand-made papers and folded fabrics can be used instead of sequins. The second column of the sampler has massed beads, crumpled silk tissue fabrics and sequins stitched down with rough and smooth gold purl. The third column shows differing arrangements of stitched beads and sequins and a motif incorporating cake-decorating mesh.

Beads can also be stitched to edges, as in diagram 27. Here, the white beads are attached to the edge in alternating horizontal and vertical alignments. Beads and sequins can be stitched singly or in clusters to form tassels and fringes, as shown in diagram 28.

In diagram 29 beads are suspended horizontally within V-shaped cuts, with a vertical wire. This arrangement can be seen in purse *b* on page 62.

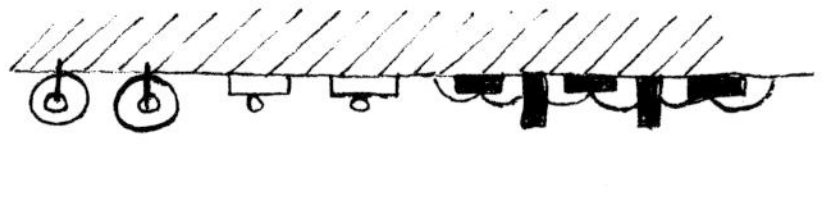

Diagram 27

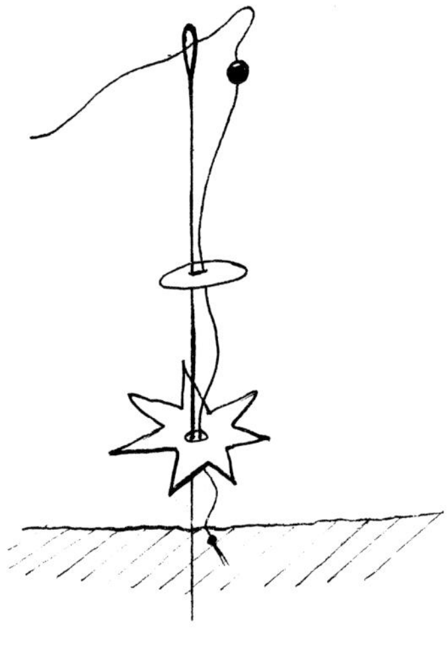

Diagram 26

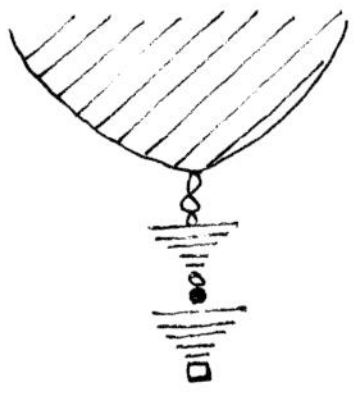

Diagram 28

Diagram 29

BEAD SAMPLER
Beads can be piled, grouped or clustered, or can be combined with sequins, paper, card, wood, stiffened or folded fabrics or with metallic thread of all kinds.

TASSELS SAMPLER
As with all new techniques, it is always best to practice or sample first before making the finished item. Tassels can be made in a variety of threads, cords, braids and yarns and experimenting with combinations of these can bring exciting results. The examples shown here have been made with embroidery threads, torn rag strips and bonded, frayed silk. This sampler shows how different tassels can look, made with the same method, but using different materials. The top row has finger tassels using braid, silk knitting yarn, and twisted and silk threads. The second row of four rag tassels incorporates cut and torn strips of silk, threads and ribbons. The third row features bonded tassels, incorporating wooden skewers and beads, and frayed shot silks.

PVA-stiffened silk

Beads or plaques can be made with hand-painted or dyed silk by pasting it with a mixture of water and PVA glue. The solution should be the consistency of thin cream. Spread the silk out on a sheet of plastic. Paste it with the mixture, making sure the liquid has soaked right through to the reverse. Hang out to dry, weighting the lower edge with pegs if there is any wind. When dry, cut into squares or triangles. The dilute glue will slightly darken the colour of the silk and will prevent fraying. The edges of the squares can be dipped in metallic fabric paint for further decoration. The pieces can be used flat, rolled up to form beads, or combined with decorated skewers and beads as in the purse on pages 94 and 97.

Tassels

Rag tassels

Rag tassels are perhaps the simplest to make. Old Indian silk scarves, washed cotton scraps or organzas, whether plain or patterned, can all be torn or cut into strips, about 2cm (3/4in) wide. Cut a selection of these into 13cm (5in) lengths and pile them together. Fold in half and bind them with a contrasting thread or yarn, just below the fold. Slip the end of the thread through a needle and pass it up through the binding and the fold, perhaps through a bead as well, and stitch to the purse.

There are many variations of the rag tassel – as many as your imagination will allow. For instance, instead of torn fabric, lengths of braid or rouleaux could be used. A bead could be threaded on each end of each piece of braid, say 15cm (6in) long, and the braid ends knotted, then halved, bound and attached.

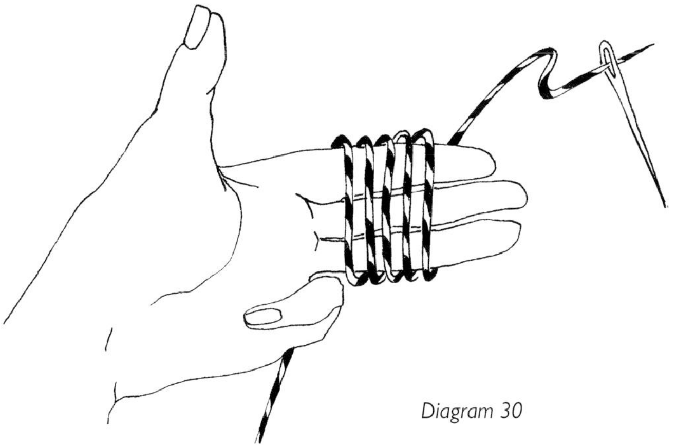

Diagram 30

Diagram 31

Looped finger tassels

Any yarn, thread, thin ribbon or braid can be used to make a finger tassel. Start with a length of say, 150cm (60in). Thread one end through a needle and wrap the other end around three fingers to within 10cm (4in) of the needle (see diagram 30). Pinch the loops on top of the index finger and slide them off. Wrap the remaining cord around three or four times and pass the needle under the wrapping and up through the loops at the top, as shown in diagram 31.

Twisted tassels

Twisted tassels can be made directly on the item to be decorated. Using a double thread and small beads, first anchor the thread to the item. Thread the first bead, hold it 2.5cm (1in) away from the purse and twist the thread until it takes up the twist with the bead in the end. Make a small holding stitch in the fabric and repeat the process until a bunch of beads are suspended by twisted threads (see diagram 32).

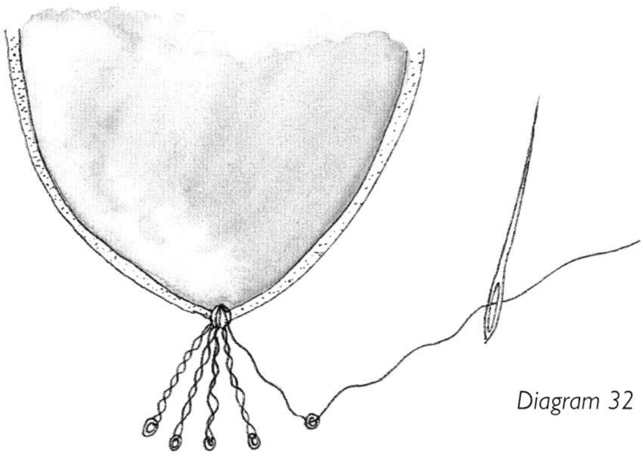

Diagram 32

Bonded, folded tassels

These are made by first bonding two fabrics together. Contrasting silk or cotton pieces are fine, perhaps one plain and the other patterned. Set the machine to a short zigzag stitch and, using machine embroidery threads, stitch a double grid of triangles or squares (see diagram 33). Cut between the lines of zigzag stitching, fold the corners over and secure with a stitch, as shown in diagram 34. Several of these tassels in a bunch could be stitched to a purse, or a single one with a loop could be used as a fastening. Examples of these tassels can be seen on page 114.

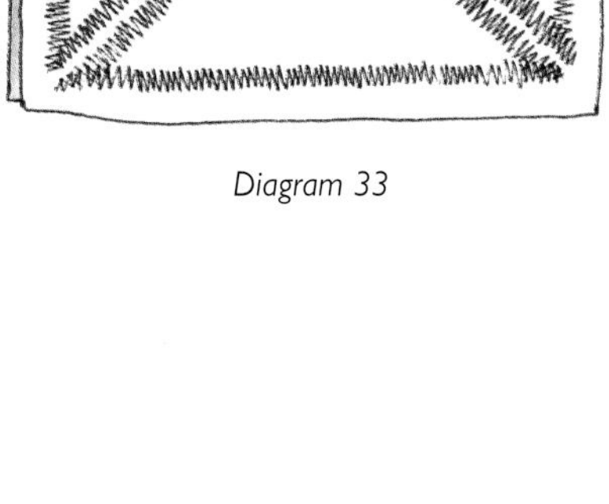

Diagram 33

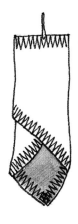

Diagram 34

Bonded and frayed tassels

Frayed tassels can look particularly spectacular when made with shot silk. A shot silk with yellow weft threads and pink warp threads will yield a yellow tassel 'body' with a gorgeous pink fringe. To make a tassel as seen in the tassel sampler, take a piece of shot silk measuring 4 x 2cm ($1\frac{1}{2}$ x $\frac{3}{4}$in). Iron a piece of Bondaweb (Wonder-Under), measuring 2 x 1.5cm ($\frac{3}{4}$ x $\frac{1}{2}$in) to one short edge, as shown in diagram 35. Fray the free edge, using a needle to tease out the weft threads. Remove the paper backing and fold into three, as shown in diagram 36, securing the shape by touching with an iron. The flat section of the tassel can be further embellished with beads (see diagram 37). Alternatively, instead of folding, the tassel can be rolled around a wooden skewer and secured by gently rolling it under an iron. Cut off the excess stick and secure the tassel to the purse with a tiny dot of glue before oversewing by hand (see diagram 38).

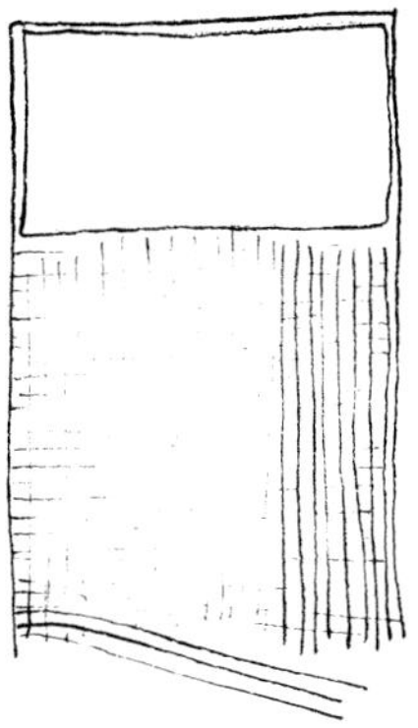

Diagram 35

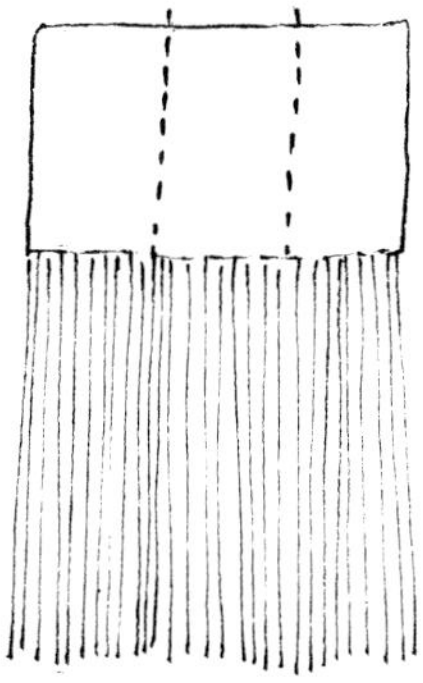

Diagram 36

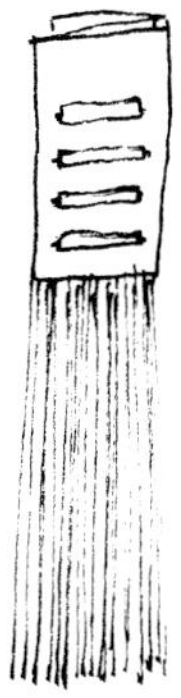

Diagram 37

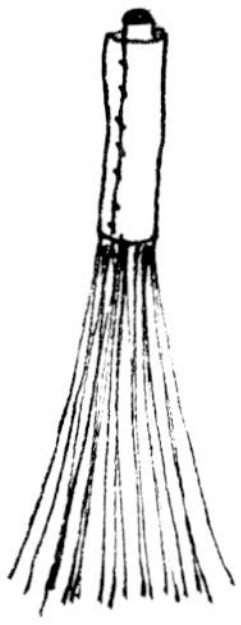

Diagram 38

Tassels from merino wool tops

Reminiscent of strapless ballgowns with tight-fitting bodices, these tassels are very easy to make. Take a length of merino top wool (produced in long 'sausages' for felt-making) and a shiny thread in a contrasting colour. Thread a large needle on the thread and wrap the other end around the top, about 2.5cm (1in) from the end. Secure by passing the needle through the binding. Cut the merino top about 1cm ($\frac{3}{8}$ in) the other side of the binding. Merino tops tassels feature on the harlequin purse on page 86.

Techniques

English patchwork

Cut triangles, squares, hexagons, octagons or diamonds from backing paper. Good-quality tracing paper or thin cartridge is best. Accuracy is essential. Chose a medium-to-light weight of cotton or Habotai silk. The weight of the fabric will be determined by the size of the templates and the purpose of the patchwork. Place the paper template on the wrong side of the fabric patch. Fold one side over and pin (see diagram 39). Fold the corner over as shown and pin (see diagram 40). Next, fold the second corner and side, as shown in diagram 41, then the final side. Tack (baste) all around. Repeat for the other patches and press on the wrong side.

To assemble, place two patches right sides together and oversew the edges as shown in diagram 42. When all the patches have been stitched together, remove the papers carefully and press the patchwork on the wrong side.

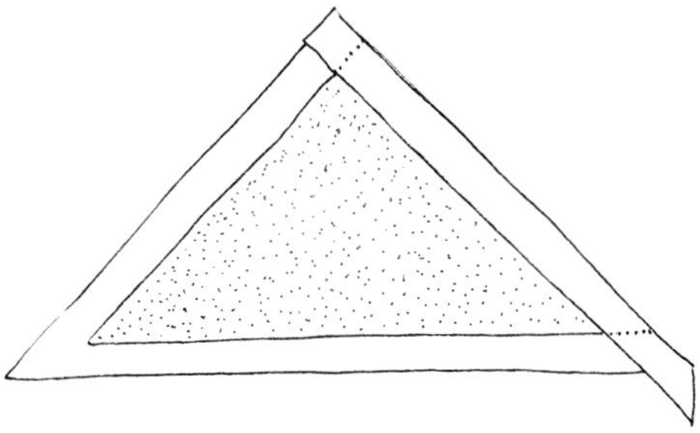

Diagram 39

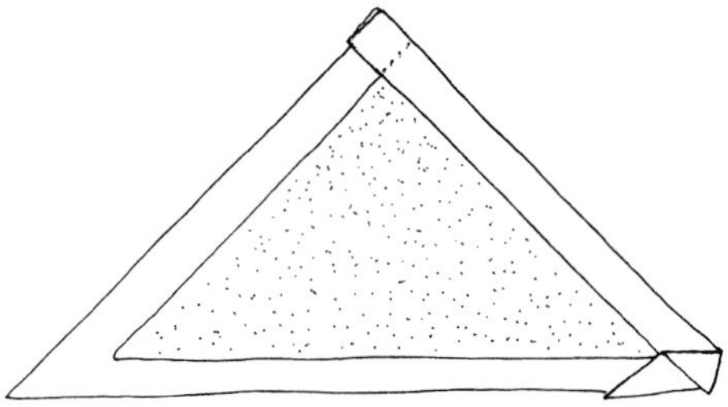

Diagram 40

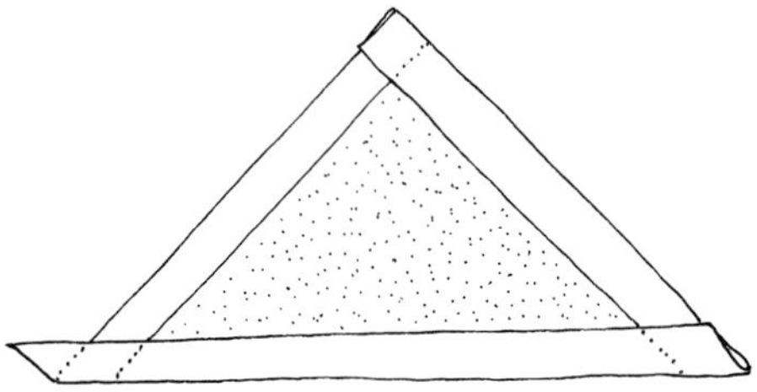

Diagram 41

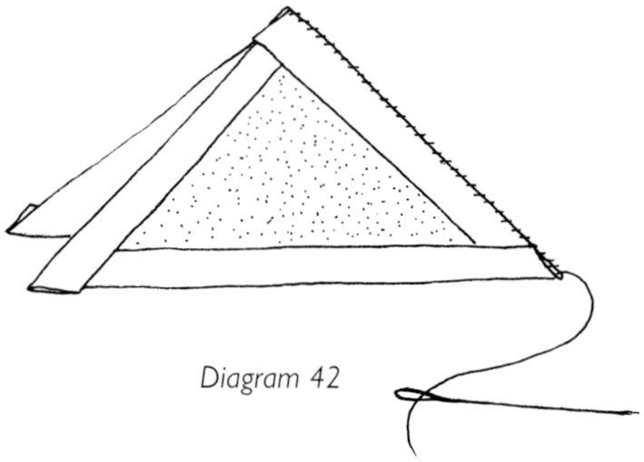

Diagram 42

Seminole patchwork

To make a piece of Seminole patchwork as in the purse on page 38, take two pieces of white cotton or silk, each 30 x 20cm (12 x 8in), and a strip of black fabric, 30 x 3cm (12 x 1 1/4in) wide. Seam a white piece to each side of the black fabric, using 1cm (3/8in) seam allowances, as in diagram 43. Press the seams open. Using a ruler, draw and make eight cuts at various angles and of varying widths. Rearrange the resulting nine strips by turning and staggering them. Seam the strips together and press the seams open; trim (see diagram 44).

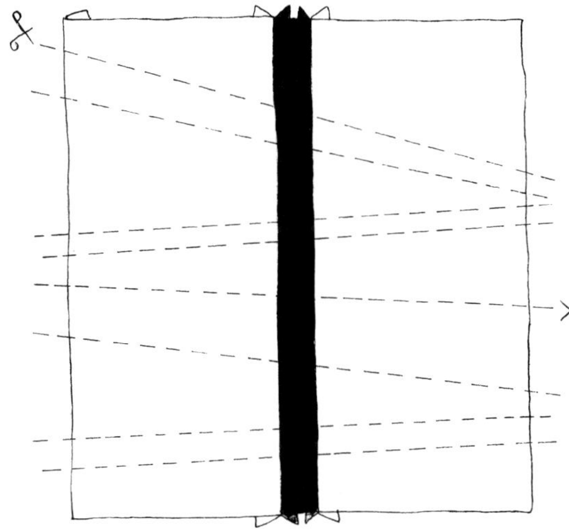

Diagram 43

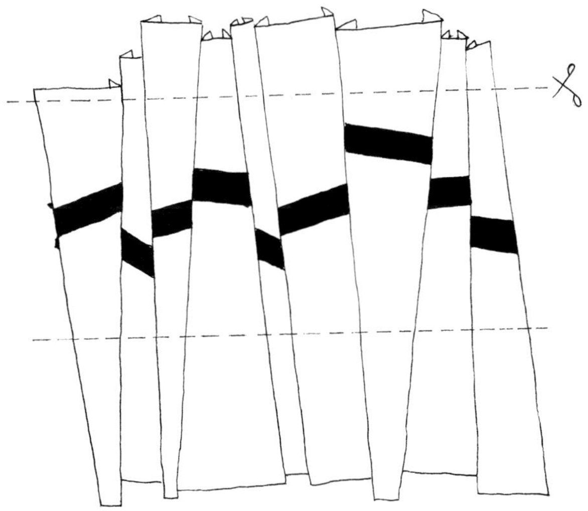

Diagram 44

Making lace on a sewing machine

Machined lace is achieved using soluble fabric and free machine embroidery techniques. It is advisable to practice free machine embroidery on a firm fabric, such as calico, initially. Cold-water-soluble fabric was used for the lace on the purse on page 52. This is a thin plastic, semi-transparent film that must be stretched taut in a bound embroidery frame. Invert the frame so that the film is flat on the machine bed. Set the stitch length and width at 0. Lower or cover the feed dog, depending on your type of machine. Remove the foot and put the presser foot down. Bring the bobbin thread to the surface by taking one stitch manually. By moving the hoop slowly while machining quite quickly, fluid movements can result in 'machine-drawn' lines.

The lace effects look good when metallic threads are used on both the bobbin and the top so that they can be seen on both sides. Machine a lacy edge, making sure that all the lines of stitching connect up, otherwise they will unravel when the fabric is dissolved. When the machining is complete, cut away the excess soluble fabric and plunge the stitching into cold water. The soluble fabric will disappear and the lace may need to be held under a running tap for a few moments. Pin the lace out on a towel to restore its shape. The real benefit of making your own lace is that it can be whatever size and colour you choose.

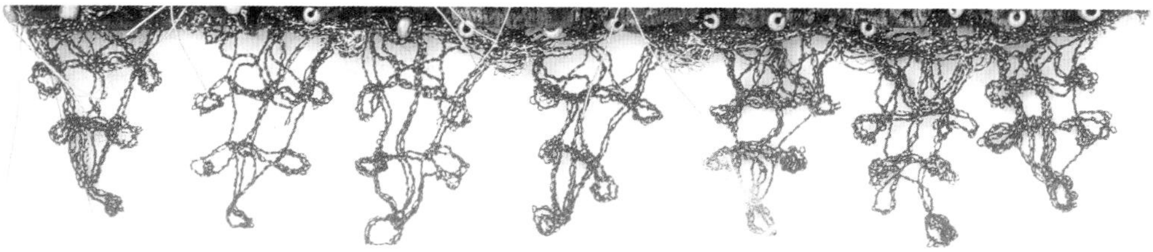

Multi-coloured canvaswork

Take canvas or closely woven linen (or indeed any material with an even weave). The canvas used in the purse on page 82 had 22 holes to the inch. Tear, cut or rip pieces of coloured net or organza and layer the pieces diagonally over the canvas. Tack (baste) through the layers and the canvas, making sure that the canvas is still visible through the layers. Using space-dyed threads, stitch a simple all-over pattern.

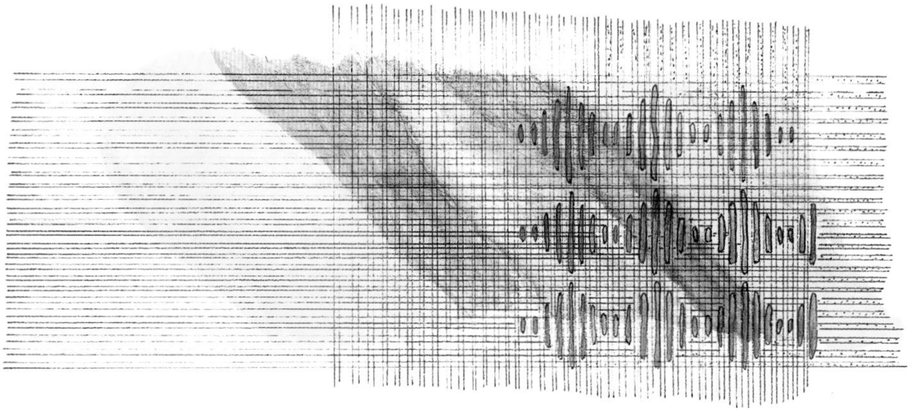

Stitches

A variety of embroidery stitches can be used as decoration on purses. Here are some of the most popular:

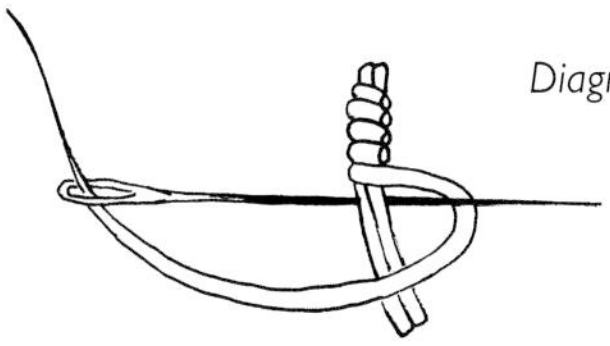

Diagram 45 ■ Buttonhole bar

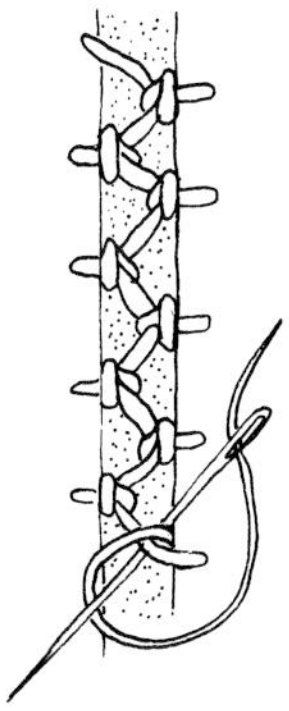

Diagram 46 ■ Insertion stitch

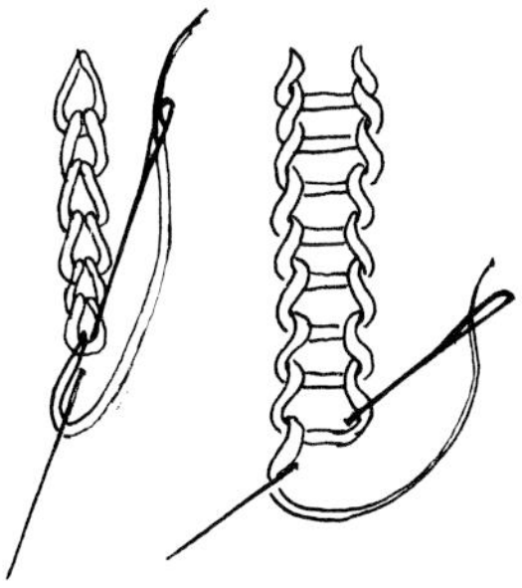

Diagram 47 ■ Two types of chain stitch

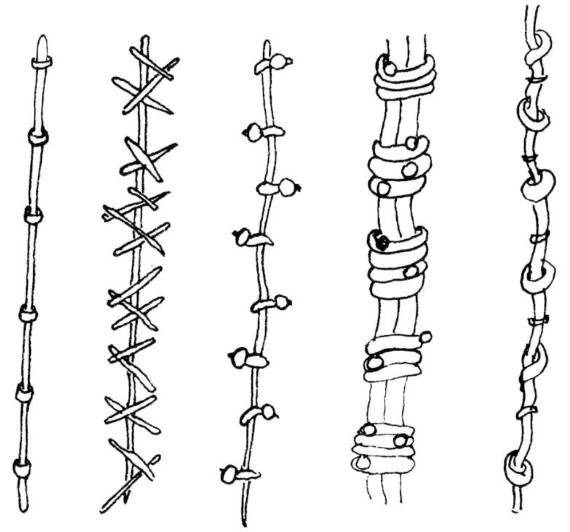

Diagram 48 ■ A variety of couching stitches

Fastenings

Beads, buttons, ties, tassels and tabs can all be used to fasten openings in purses. The diagrams on these pages show just a few of the possibilities.

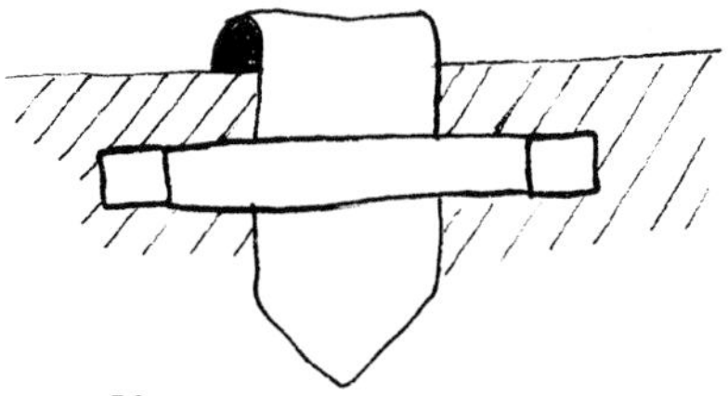

Diagram 50

Diagram 49: A loop fits neatly around a bead or button.

Diagram 50: A tab of fabric is brought over from the back of the purse and passes through a band on the front.

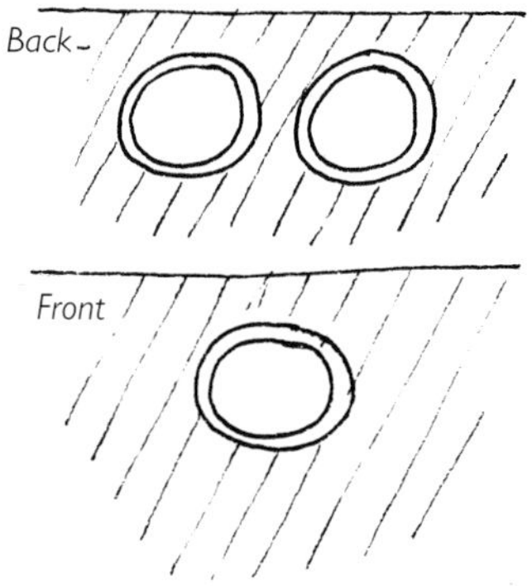

Diagram 51

Diagrams 51 and 52: Two bound circles, cut in the back of the purse, line up with a similarly cut and bound circle on the front. A wooden skewer or piece of shaped bamboo is threaded through the front hole and between the back two holes.

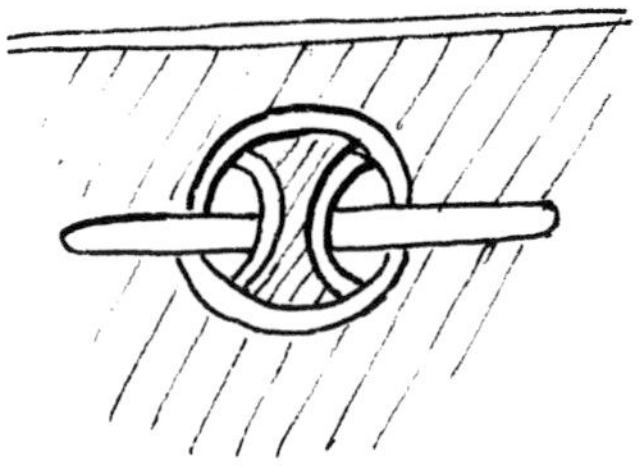

Diagram 52

Diagrams 53 and 54: A cord, brought forward from the back of the purse, wraps around a button sewn onto the front. Alternatively, two buttons attached one above the other on the purse flap and the purse front are wound in a figure of eight with a cord.

Diagram 55: A tassel on the front of the purse threads through a loop on the back.

Diagram 56: A spiral of ribbon stitched on the back of a purse folds forward over a bead on the front.

Diagram 57: An octagonal piece of card with a square hole cut in the middle is buttonholed all round and attached to the purse (see photograph on page 82). A cord handle is threaded through.

Diagrams 58 and 59: Ties on the front and back knot at the top of the purse.

Diagram 49

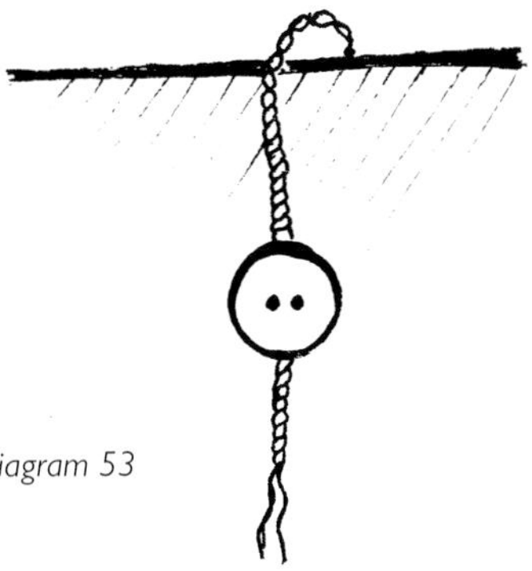

Diagram 53

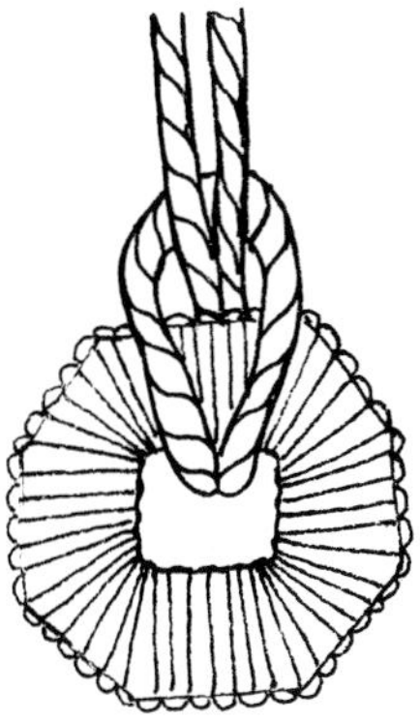

Diagram 57

Diagram 54

Diagram 58

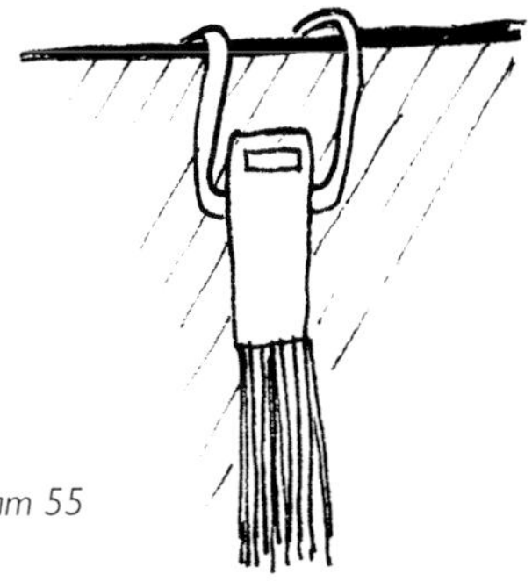

Diagram 55

Diagram 59

Diagram 56

CONCLUSION

We can learn much about the construction of purses by making drawings of antique items in museums, or by collecting purses from around the world and studying them. Their variety and sheer opulence never ceases to amaze.

The possibilities for us as makers are endless. Many of the purses in this book could be adapted in very different ways. The black-and-white purses at the beginning of the book, for example, could be made in vibrant colours; their dimensions could be altered or they could be given shaped gussets, completely changing their forms.

Highly coloured purses, such as those inspired by Elizabethan textiles, could be made in monochrome with an emphasis on texture. What would the Marine Life purse on page 78 look like if it were made in linen, with monochrome embroidery in silk thread and a long, linen thread tassel? What would the Harlequin purse on page 86 look like if it were created with a machine-embroidered surface instead of a patched one?

Alternative design sources and other techniques from the vast array available to the modern embroiderer, along with individual imaginations and skills, will no doubt result in original, personal and unique purses.

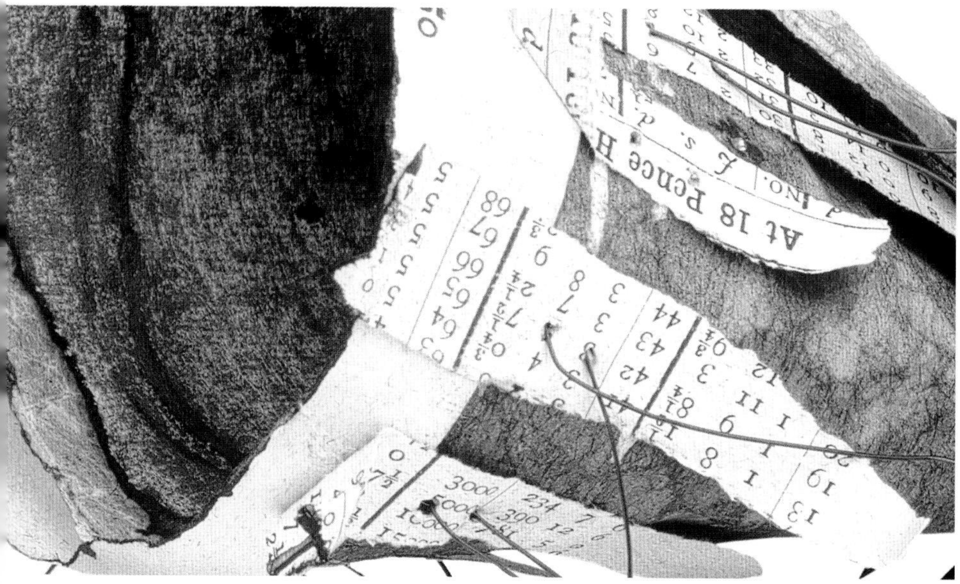

JAN MILLER'S PURSE
Torn fragments of text, linen, wire and paper are layered and folded together to create an evocation of childhood memories (see page 64).

PURSE COLLECTIONS

It is always advisable to contact museums to find out what they have on display at any given time. Most will give you an appointment to see a specific article in their collection.

The Embroiderers' Guild
Apartment 41
Hampton Court Palace
Surrey
KT8 9AU
Tel: 020 8943 1229
www.embroiderersguild.com

The Victoria and Albert Museum
South Kensington
London
SW7 2RL
Tel: 020 7942 2275
www.vam.ac.uk

Guildford Museum
Castle Arch
Guildford
Surrey
GU1 3SE
Tel: 01483 444 750
www.guildfordmuseum.co.uk

Rachel Kay-Shuttleworth Collection
Gawthorpe Hall
Padiham
Burnley
Lancashire
BB12 8UA
Tel: 01282 771 004

Museum of London
London Wall
London
EC21 5HN
Tel: 020 7600 3699
www.museumoflondon.org.uk

Museum of Bags and Purses
Zonnestein 1
1181 LR Amsterdam
Tel: 0031 20 6478681
www.museumofbagsandpurses.com

The Museum of Fine Arts, Boston
Avenue of the Arts
465 Huntingdon Avenue
Boston, MA 02115-5597
USA
Tel: 001 617 267 9300
www.mfa.org

A PURSE FROM SPAIN
This purse, measuring 18cm (7in) wide and 14cm (5½in) long has been made from a reused textile. Stems, flowers and leaves are embroidered in silk and laid metal threads on cream silk, and the purse is edged with metal lace and braid. The drawstring is made with twisted metal and silk threads. The lining is blue silk with an interlining of paper, which has probably contributed to the delicate state of the purse. (Embroiderers' Guild)

SUPPLIERS

Art Van Go
The Studios
1 Stevenage Road
Knebworth
Hertfordshire
SG3 6AN
Tel: 01438 814 946
www.artvango.co.uk
Fabric paints, papers, dyes

Freudenberg Nonwovens LP
Lowfields Business Park
Elland
West Yorkshire
HX5 5DX
Tel: 01422 327 900
www.vilene.com

Freudenberg Nonwovens Pellon
3440 Industrial Drive
Durham, NC 27704
USA
Bondaweb (Wonder-Under) and pelmet Vilene

Mace and Nairn
PO Box 5626
Northampton
NN7 2BF
Tel: 01604 864 924
www.maceandnairn.com
Substitute jap gold

The Scientific Wire Company
18 Raven Road
London
E18 1HW
Tel: 020 8505 0002
www.wires.co.uk
Coloured wires

The Silk Route
Cross Cottage
Cross Lane
Frimley Green
Surrey
GU16 6LN
Tel: 01252 835 781
www.thesilkroute.co.uk
Silk, silk tissue fabrics, dupion, organzas.

Variegations
Rose Cottage
Harper Royd Lane
Norland
Halifax
West Yorkshire
HX6 3QQ
Tel: 01422 832 411
www.variegations.com
Velvets, wool tops, variegated threads and tubular ribbons

BIBLIOGRAPHY

Benn, Elizabeth. *Treasures from the Embroiderers' Guild.* David and Charles, 1991
Cumming, Valerie. *The Visual History of Costume Accessories.* B T Batsford, 1998
Edwards, Joan. *Bead Embroidery.* Lacis, 1966
Foster, Vanda. *Bags and Purses.* B T Batsford, 1982
Johnson, Anna. *Handbags: The Power of the Purse.* Workman Publishing, 2002
Johnson, Eleanor. *Fashion Accessories.* Shire, 1983
Leber, Judith. *The Artful Handbag.* Abrams, 1995
Lemon, Jane. *Embroidered Boxes.* B T Batsford, 2003
Littlejohn, Jean. *Voluptuous Velvet.* Double Trouble Enterprises, 1997
Staniland, Kay. *Medieval Craftsmen: Embroiderers.* British Museum Press, 1991
Wang, Loretta H. *The Chinese Purse.* Hilit Publishing Co. Ltd., 1991
Wilcox, Claire. *Bags and Purses.* V&A publications, 1991
Yarong, Wang. *Chinese Folk Embroidery.* Thames and Hudson, 1987

INDEX